Moses & Son

Pioneers of Frontier Florida

Jerald Blizin

Copyright © 2017 Jerald Blizin

All rights reserved.

ISBN: 1542304210
ISBN-13: 978-1542304214

For Joe —
whose flying fingers
made this book possible!
(and for Donna + Turbo, too)
Best,
Jerry

CONTENTS

Introduction	1
Chapter 1	5
Chapter 2	14
Chapter 3	21
Chapter 4	26
Chapter 5	34
Chapter 6	41
Chapter 7	51
Chapter 8	57
Chapter 9	64
Chapter 10	75
Chapter 11	85
Chapter 12	92
Chapter 13	100
Chapter 14	105
Chapter 15	117
Chapter 16	127
Bibliography	131
About the Author	136

INTRODUCTION

Three hundred and twenty-five years after the Jews were expelled from Spain, Moses Elias Levy, a 36-year-old Sephardic Jew devised a plan that would make Florida a homeland for the displaced Jews of the world. It was fitting irony. Florida had been held by the Spaniards twice over periods that stretched back to the 16th century.

In 1817, when Moses Levy formulated his plan, the Inquisition still held sway in the New World. Exported to the West Indies in 1511, the Inquisition was still in force as late as 1848. As a colonial power, however, Spain was considerably weakened when it began talking seriously with the U.S. over the sale of Florida.

Levy himself was an anomaly. Of Portuguese descent, his father had been grand vizier to the ruler of Morocco, where Moses Levy was born in 1781 under the family name of Yulee. He subsequently dropped the name in favor of Levy, claiming it was too cumbersome for business. Levy was his mother's maiden name. The family had to flee Morocco to Gibraltar after the emperor died.

At age 19, Moses Levy emigrated from Gibraltar to the island of St. Thomas and soon became a prosperous lumber dealer. He remained a resident for the next 16 years, during which time the island passed from British to Danish possession.

He married and sired four children, but the marriage failed. In1816, divorced and unhappy, Levy moved to Havana. Despite his Jewishness he supplied the Spanish army garrisoned in Cuba. Doubtless his Danish citizenship conferred some immunity on him, for no overt harm befell him from the Spanish.

Aware of the impending sale of Florida to the United States, he began to negotiate with a Spaniard in Florida, Don Fernando de la Maza Arredondo, who had been granted 289,000 acres in the central part of the state. Through trade and outright purchase, he was able to acquire substantial acreage, so that by the time cession of Florida took place, Moses Levy owned 52,900 acres.

This story tells of his successes and failures, his 33-year residency in America, and his contributions to the development of Florida as well as to American Judaism, at a time when the existence of this faith in the new nation was tenuous at best. Not only did Moses E. Levy plan a Jewish homeland in Florida, he proposed in 1821 to establish the first Jewish boarding school in the country.

This story also tells of the contributions of Moses Levy's youngest son, David Levy Yulee, who led wilderness Florida into statehood and became its first U.S. Senator of Jewish descent, as well as its first successful cross-state railroad builder.

As politician and entrepreneur, David Levy Yulee's career was as remarkable as his father's. Both father and son epitomize opposite sides of the Jewish experience in America--the father a zealously observant Jew; the son a secular and assimilated American.

At the time of statehood, David Levy was the most powerful political figure in Florida. But just before going to the U.S. Senate in 1845, he chose to change his last name to Yulee. He remains to this day the only person in Florida to have had his name changed by an act of the legislature. This action was triggered by a controversy between him and his religious father, one which had grown bitter as a result of David's decision to study law and seek a career in politics. Both David and an older brother, Elias, broke communication with their father.

Yet it was the turbulent world of politics which eventually helped father and son find a pathway to reconciliation. David, who turned away from his Jewish roots, was to be politically attacked because of them--bitter attacks that preceded the Civil War and followed it during the long agony over secession and slavery. Moses Levy rose to defend his son against what he called "unspeakable lies."

For more than 23 years during his career as a public official, David Levy Yulee endured the slurs of anti-Semitism. At the outset of his career, he was falsely labeled an "alien." At the summit, he was openly smeared as a "treacherous Jew." And yet Florida's frontier society had been open enough to permit him to rise to high political position.

Moses Levy's dream of building a New Jerusalem in Florida did not succeed. The school plan also failed. David Levy Yulee built the first major railroad line uniting the Atlantic and Gulf coasts of the state--only to see his years of work dashed by the Civil War. The war shattered the railroad shortly after it began full operation.

Although David Levy Yulee defended slavery he became a reluctant secessionist who did not participate in the Confederate government. Nevertheless, he was jailed for alleged acts of treason and was confined for nine months without ever being tried for a crime. He was released only after Ulysses S. Grant wrote President Andrew Johnson.

The cross-Florida railroad became David Yulee's obsession--he tried to save it from confiscation by carpet-baggers, even Salmon P. Chase, chief justice of the Supreme Court, and from creditors. He fought governors and state legislators who tried to change the rail line's route. For 20 years after the Civil War he labored to restore the health of his railroad, finally selling his interests and moving back to Washington, D.C. at age 71. He died in 1886 after catching cold on a steamboat en route to New York City.

Moses Levy had displayed the same kind of tenacity. Though unable to establish a Jewish homeland in Florida, he established many plantations and became a leading citizen of the old Spanish city of St. Augustine. He never ceased to confront those who attacked Judaism. He died in 1854 while visiting a Virginia spa. Though he had reconciled with David at the time of his death, it took 60 years to straighten out his will.

Moses and son nevertheless found fulfillment in Florida. Optimists and persevering loners, they built their dreams on the ashes of Spain's abandoned empire. Descendants of persecuted people, they proved that in the New World opportunity awaited those with the energy and drive to seize it. Deep within both men were the strongest instincts of survival. In their respective American experiences each was always his own man.

1

Moses Elias Levy arrived at the island of St. Thomas in the year 1800. He had sailed from his home in Gibraltar as supercargo aboard a merchant ship delivering timber and other supplies. The 19-year-old lad had been lucky to arrive intact, for he had nearly been crushed to death on the ship when a stack of timber shifted. But it was all part of life on the razor's edge, which had been the family's lot for years.

Moses Levy was, in 1800, like many Jews of Portuguese descent looking for a country in which to live peacefully and prosper. The islands of the Caribbean offered that opportunity. His journey to St. Thomas thus stemmed from a long and intricate chain of events.

He was born July 11, 1781 at Mogador, Morocco, where his father was grand vizier to the emperor. The father had always served the emperor well. But one day he discovered a plot by the crown prince to overthrow the old ruler. As a result, the ambitious prince was thrown in prison. When the emperor died and the prince took the throne, the grand vizier and his family were forced to flee to Gibraltar.

By then the family included two children, Moses Elias and his sister, Rachel. They were not "Mahometans" as Moses Levy's grandson was to claim many years later but professing Jews, like many of Sephardic origin who had gone to North Africa after expulsion from Spain and Portugal.

Although the family's last name in Morocco had been Yulee, Moses Elias Levy declined to use it as a businessman in St. Thomas because it was too "cumbrous." It appears that the original impetus to use Levy as a family name came from Moses' English-born mother. It was her maiden name. Nevertheless, Moses Levy occasionally used Yulee as a pen name in America. He often wrote letters to newspapers--sometimes signing as "Eulee" or "Youlee."

Besides, as he wrote in a letter of Feb. 24, 1846 to the Florida Herald and Southern Democrat, "surnames (sic) are little thought of by Orientals. A Levite with the Jews is called but Levy."

True enough. Jews for centuries had no last names. They were often identified in Iberia by their city or place of residence. During the Inquisition, when Jews were forced to convert, they were frequently given new surnames like "Salvador" (savior) or "Santangel" (sainted angel. When Sephardic Jews began to immigrate to America in the 17th century some still bore these "converso" names while others had common Hispanic names like Nunez or Garcia.

The financiers of Columbus' first voyage were forced converts- Luis de Santangel, chancellor and comptroller of Aragon and his brother-in-law, Gabriel Sanchez, the court treasurer. As many as five conversos were on the voyage, including interpreter Luis de Torres, the first man ashore on San Salvador.

In ancient times, Jews were classed either as Levites or Cohens (priests). Thus, the ancestral names of Cohen and Levy have come down through the centuries.

Though there were quite a few Levys in 19th century America they were frequently unrelated. At least 15 Levy families were documented in America prior to 1840. Some writers contend that Yulee was an honorary title in Morocco rather than a family name but Moses Levy himself told his lawyer that his full name in Morocco was Moses Elias Levy Yulee.

While his wife and two children settled in Gibraltar after the flight from Morocco, the senior Yulee went back to North Africa, probably to seek re-employment. He died in Egypt under unknown circumstances. Since several Muslim rulers in North Africa employed Jews as financial advisers and diplomats at this time, it is reasonable to conclude that Yulee was actively seeking new work.

Moses Elias Levy arrived in St. Thomas to find a small but thriving Jewish community. His co-religionists, in fact, had taken root all over the Caribbean wherever Hispanic influence was absent. Jews could be found on Dutch islands like Curacao or on British possessions, such as Jamaica or the Bahamas. St. Thomas was first a British, then a Danish island before becoming part of the U.S. Virgin Islands.

Having expelled their Jews, both Spain and Portugal also exported their inquisition to the New World so that Jews remained unwelcome in most Iberian possessions. In fact, the first 25 Jews who reached New Amsterdam in 1654 were refugees from Recife, Brazil, a Dutch colony which had been recaptured by the Portuguese.

In the tolerant atmosphere of St. Thomas, Moses Elias married a Jewish woman, Hannah Abendanone, and soon fathered four children: Elias, Rahma, Rachel and David. Levy's mother and sister traveled from Gibraltar to Puerto Rico and then to St. Thomas, where they also settled. His sister Rachel married Joseph Benlisa in St. Thomas, where she remained the rest of her life. Moses became a successful lumber dealer and a partner in the firm of Levy, Benjamin and Robles.

There were many Benjamins in the islands. Moses Levy's partner was most likely Emanuel Benjamin of St. Thomas rather than Philip Benjamin of St. Croix, the father of future southern statesman Judah P. Benjamin. Emanuel Benjamin once held a mortgage on Moses Levy's house and records disclose he had other business dealings with M.E. Levy. He was an uncle of Judah P. Benjamin.

Moses Elias Levy's other partner, Solomon Judah Robles, remained in the background, though it is known that he died on a trip to America in 1816.

Moses' daughters, Rahma and Rachel, stayed on St. Thomas and married well; Rahma married Jonathan da Costa and Rachel married Abraham P.

Henriques. Both were planters. The da Costa sons, Dr. Joseph Mendes da Costa, and Charles da Costa, earned fame respectively in Philadelphia and New York. Dr. Joseph Mendes da Costa was professor of medicine at Jefferson Medical College in Philadelphia, while Charles da Costa was prominent in the New York Bar and was a trustee of Columbia College. Both became Episcopalians.

As he prospered, Moses Levy increasingly became a more ardent Jew. He found the casualness of the Jewish community to be "an eyesore" and he took a literal and fundamentalist view of the Old Testament.

According to the writings of his son, David, this fervent religiosity was a primary cause of the breakup of Moses' marriage to Hannah in 1815. Yet there were other unspecified problems. The couple lived apart for three years, according to the divorce papers.

David spent his first nine years on St. Thomas, where he was born on June 2, 1810. Though he remembered seeing the flags on St. Thomas change from British to Danish his other recollections of the island were fuzzy. He only returned once, for a brief visit, as a youth.

The author of a scholarly dissertation, Joseph Gary Adler, contends that Moses Levy was an adherent of the radical Karaite sect, which rejected the interpretations of the Talmud and interpreted the Old Testament literally. Whatever the facts, he could write Hebrew characters and knew his Bible. He was also inclined to publish brochures in defense of the Jews, as well as engage in debate.

While in Europe some years later, he published a pamphlet titled "Letter Concerning the Present Condition of the Jews, Being a Correspondence Between Mr. Forster and Mr. Levy." The pamphlet covered a three-year correspondence between Levy and Forster. Another pamphlet was published at York, England, regarding a "controversy" between Levy and one Capt. Thomas Thrush of the Royal Navy on the subject of Judaism.

In 1816, Moses Levy departed St. Thomas for Havana, leaving behind his former wife and children. Here, despite his very clear Jewish origins, he became a supplier to the Spanish military in Cuba. Moses Levy apparently was protected from inquisitional authority by his Danish citizenship. He was clearly a well-connected trader and, as sometimes happens, Spanish military authorities were less concerned with religion than they were with having a reliable source of supply.

Though Spain was a weakened power by 1816, the inquisition had not vanished. It had been exported to the West Indies in 1511 and to other colonies by 1576. During the Passover of 1554 in Mexico City, 80 Jews and a number of Indians were killed in an auto-da-fe. Other persecutions persisted until 1848 in Spanish colonies.

Levy was always a man with his eyes and ears open for opportunity.

In 1817, when U.S. acquisition of Florida seemed imminent, he bought property in east Florida. He had to deal with the original grantees because no Jew could buy or be granted land directly from the Spanish. In fact, a condition for any Spanish grant in Florida was that the recipient swear loyalty to His Catholic Majesty and agree to raise his children as Catholics. By deciding to buy, Moses Levy thus was walking into one of the most politically charged real estate arenas in the world.

The once-powerful Spaniards had become worn and weary occupiers of the unruly peninsula by 1817. Americans contended that if Spain couldn't rule Florida, they should give it up.

The U.S. had considered acquiring Florida since 1779. In 1799 Alexander Hamilton had declared acquisition of Louisiana and Florida "essential to the permanency of the union." Thomas Jefferson had authorized negotiations to buy Louisiana and Florida simultaneously.

Though Louisiana was subsequently acquired from France, the U.S. failed to buy Florida when it had a chance. Nobody seemed sure of the exact boundaries, even though President James Madison proclaimed that west Florida, from the Perdido to the Mississippi, had been part of the Louisiana Purchase.

In 1811 Congress secretly authorized the president to peacefully occupy Florida to prevent seizure by a foreign power. Next, the territory became a frequent target of assorted adventurers for seizure from the Spaniards. A patriot army took Amelia Island in 1812, apparently having been given secret assurances by President Madison and Congress that the U.S. would accept the island. Instead the takeover was repudiated.

In 1817, a Scottish adventurer named Gregor Macgregor raised the Green Cross of Florida flag over Amelia Island, which he took from a small Spanish garrison without firing a shot. Within days, a pirate named Luis Aury claimed the island for Mexico. In the end U.S. marines had to retake the island and hold it for Spain until cession.

Andrew Jackson almost precipitated a war with Spain after James Monroe became president when he captured Pensacola in 1818 and forced the Spanish governor to surrender. Secretary of state John Quincy Adams backed Jackson, however, and pushed America's claim to Florida in tough negotiations with Spanish Ambassador Luis de Onis. This finally culminated in the Adams-Onis treaty of 1819.

However, the king of Spain threw a wrench into the works by making all sorts of last-minute Florida land grants to his courtiers, prompting Henry Clay to complain: "What do we get for Florida? We get Florida loaded and encumbered with land grants which leave scarcely a foot of soil for the United States."

Some of these grants were set aside prior to the Adams-Onis treaty whereby the U.S agreed to pay Spain a scant $5 million for Florida. European opinion was running against the acquisition and Adams, who didn't care what Europe thought, said "if the world do not hold us for Romans, they will take us for Jews, and of the two vices I would rather be charged with that which has greatness mingled in its composition."

Amidst this complex turmoil, Moses Elias Levy reasoned that this was the time to buy in Florida; the land would appreciate, and what is more, if he could acquire a substantial tract, he would establish upon it a homeland for the Jews of Europe, whom he knew to be in a "degraded" state.

To be sure, Levy was totally unaware of Adams remarks. He saw only an opportunity to help the Jews of Europe. Confined in ghettos, denied the privileges accorded ordinary citizens, the objects of brutality and oppression, the Chosen People hardly lived as Moses Levy felt they should.

By buying land the hated Spanish had held and establishing a Jewish homeland upon it, Moses Levy saw himself as an instrument of righteous retribution. Surely an all-seeing God would smile upon such a venture.

Moses Levy learned that Spanish authorities had granted 289,000 acres of land in Florida to Don Fernando de la Maza Arredondo. Arredondo had been a resident of St. Augustine in 1811 and had helped Spanish troops at that time. The grant to Arredondo was made Sept. 3, 1817. Before approaching Arredondo, Levy negotiated to purchase a tract of land near Alligator Creek in East Florida, to be paid for when Florida was formally ceded to the U.S.

When the treaty of cession was signed in 1819, Levy traded his tract for a share of the Arredondo property. Starting with a smaller purchase of some 36,000 acres, he wound up through the trade with some 52,900 acres of Florida land. His cash outlay was about $40,000.

Moses Levy's hopes for a Jewish homeland no doubt had been lifted by Article 5 of the Adams-Onis treaty, which stated "the inhabitants of the ceded territories shall be secured in the free exercise of their religion, without any restriction."

The next chapter in Moses Levy's life was about to begin.

2

In 1818, Moses Levy visited the United States. When he returned to Cuba he studied how Cuban plantations were run and decided to replicate them in America. He spent the next year in feverish preparation. In 1820 he sent word to an associate in London, Frederick Warburg, that he was ready to go ahead with colonization of his initial plantation. He purchased sugar cane, fruit trees and seeds to be sent to America.

Warburg began advertising for European Jews willing to settle at the central Florida plantation Levy would call "Pilgrimage." It was to be located near Micanopy in Alachua County, where most of Levy's holdings were centered.

Levy paused in his busy logistical operations in 1819 to bring his two sons to America for their education. Seventeen-year-old Elias was enrolled at Harvard while nine-year-old David was sent to Norfolk, Va., in the care of Moses Myers, who enrolled him in the Norfolk Academy. Levy did not bring his daughters to America.

David's passage was not without travail. According to his son, C. Wickliffe Yulee, some sailors on the ship carrying the boy engaged in horseplay which ended with David being thrown into the sea. The experience caused him to fear the water for the rest of his life. As a result he was reluctant to travel abroad. Wickliffe also said his father came to America bearing a blue scar on his forehead in the shape of a Y, the result of a fall while playing. He bore this mark all his days.

By 1821, Moses Levy was operating at full throttle. He came to Savannah and Charleston to expedite acquisition of supplies; he also travelled to New York and Philadelphia, managing to establish relationships with leading Jews of these communities.

On June 8, 1821 he appeared before the Circuit Court at Philadelphia to declare his intent to become a U.S. citizen. The application form gives us a description of the man. It read: country, Denmark; age, 40; condition, single; profession, planter; stature, 5 feet, 6 inches; hair, black; forehead, round; weight, 180 pounds; eyes, dark; nose, straight; mouth, moderate; chin, round; visage, oval.

Meanwhile, Andrew Jackson -- military governor of the Florida territory -- had issued an ordinance allowing "every free, male inhabitant of Florida on July 17, 1821" to become a citizen by making application and taking the oath.

Though the Adams-Onis treaty was concluded in 1819 it was not ratified until Feb. 22, 1821. The flags did not change over until July of that year. There was little doubt that Moses Elias Levy wanted to become a citizen. Though he did not complete the naturalization process in Philadelphia, he fully expected to be in St. Augustine before the American flag was raised early in July

He set out by stagecoach from Philadelphia to Charleston. At Charleston, he took a ship bound for St. Augustine. However, the vessel was becalmed and sat several days within sight of the Florida shore.

A court challenged the legality of Jackson's proclamation granting citizenship so on March 4, 1822, Moses Levy again applied for citizenship. He complicated things by stating he was "probably not" in Florida on July 17, 1821. Some sources theorize he became confused over the date of the change of flags, which actually took place on July 10 in St. Augustine and on July 17 at Pensacola. A certificate of citizenship was issued, however, and subsequently validated by federal court ruling.

Whatever the circumstances of his arrival, the occasion seems to have been a big social event in St. Augustine. The leading citizens of the town gave a welcoming dinner in Moses Levy's honor. It was the kind of shindig that has been repeated for two centuries in Florida whenever a developer with deep pockets has arrived to create jobs and spend money. Nobody challenged his religion, his development plans or his pedigree. Here was a man of means and with him traveled the Great God, Progress.

Several other Jews were also naturalized at the oldest Spanish city at this time, including George Levy, 26, a planter, and Lewis Solomon, 30, a watchmaker, both from London; Levy M. Rodenberg, 29, a grocer from Amsterdam and Isaac Hendricks, 47, (country of origin not known) a planter who came to Florida from South Carolina. It isn't clear whether the European Jews were Warburg recruits or arrived on their own initiative.

Levy was soon among the busiest men in Florida. He bought a coastal schooner, "The Fly." He expanded his land purchases, obtaining property from Antonio Fernandez Mier (a Jew?) as well as more acreage at Alligator Creek near the St. John's River. He bought land at Black Creek, Cedar Swamp, Cassonville and Charcola. Eight miles above Lake George, Levy planted sugar cane and built a mill, as well as a place called "Hope Hill." He spent $17,000 cutting a road through the forest from the St. Johns River to St. Augustine.

On Feb. 18, 1822, he signed an agreement to build 15 houses at "Pilgrimage," his plantation at Micanopy, where he also built a sugar mill. Levy hired Anthony Rutant to be overseer of the plantation.

Warburg had also successfully recruited some French and German settlers. The Chateauneuf family, among the French newcomers, would soon plant grapes and cultivate the vine, Levy hoped. Warburg was interested in promoting wine-production in America and had discussed this with Levy. A distant relative of the Hamburg banking family, Warburg acted primarily as a recruiting agent, however.

Moses Levy was said to be personally opposed to slavery yet came to accept what was the prevailing myth of the South--that slaves were "essential" to running a plantation. Cutting sugar cane, an arduous and uncomfortable task, was best done by Africans, it was claimed. Therefore, 15 slaves went along with the first party of 23 European settlers sent to Micanopy.

During 1823, 25 houses were erected at Micanopy and frames for 10 others were put up.

However, Moses Levy's dream of making his property a Jewish homeland abruptly ended. The Arredondo grant of 1817 required settlement by 200 families within three years. There was no way Moses Levy could get 200 Jewish families on site inside of three years, even if he had somehow acquired the financial resources of a Rothschild.

Therefore, he had instructed Warburg to find any willing Europeans as settlers, regardless of religion. The latter adjusted his recruiting advertisements accordingly. Still, some European Jews continued to respond to Warburg's solicitation.

Arredondo and his son also sold another portion of land to some New Yorkers who incorporated as the Alachua Land co. But a cloud had been hanging over the Spanish land grants for some time, including those Arredondo sold to Levy. When John Quincy Adams started negotiating for Florida he wanted to invalidate all land grants made by the Spanish king after 1802. In 1818, King Ferdinand VII made three vast grants in Florida--one to the captain of his bodyguards, another to one of his chamberlains and a third to his treasurer.

These were so large and ill timed they were annulled prior to signing of the treaty of 1819. Adams finally agreed to a cut-off date of Jan. 24, 1818 on Spanish land grants. Nevertheless, people like Andrew Jackson complained bitterly about bad faith by the Spanish government and muttered that the only response the U.S. ought to make to Spain was from the "mouth of a cannon." It was the land grant flap which delayed treaty implementation for better than a year.

Suits were later filed alleging that the entire Arredondo grant was invalid. Judge Joseph L. Smith of the Superior Court for East Florida ruled the grant valid in November of 1830, but the issue was to remain tangled until the Supreme Court upheld Judge Smith. The grant to Arredondo was made in 1817, well within the permitted period.

However, in 1849 the Arredondo grant was ordered sold at auction to clear the title and Moses Levy had to buy his land all over again. He had established claim to 34,175 acres but bid in 49,692 acres, paying $17,145.83.

Attorney General William Wirt (who was to end up as a would-be Florida land developer himself) appointed a special counsel to look into the legality of the Arredondo property (and other grants) prior to the court rulings. Investigators were sent to Cuba to look into the records, which the Spanish seemed reluctant to disclose. Surveys apparently had never been properly done and the documentation in Spanish was also unclear to the Americans.

One of the investigators was Richard Keith Call, a disciple of Andrew Jackson who later became territorial delegate and twice governor of Florida. Call was angered by the court rulings upholding the validity of the grant. He believed the whole deal was fraudulent.

The legal upheaval was upsetting--and expensive--for Moses Levy. Litigation cast a cloud over his property for years. And there were more troubles. The plantation at Micanopy was in the very center of Seminole Indian country. In fact, the name Micanopy is that of the Seminole chief who led the Dade Massacre, in which virtually all but three members of a 103-man column of troops marching from Ft. Brooke (Tampa) to Ft. King (Ocala) were wiped out by warring Seminoles in December, 1835.

One of Florida's epic battles with the Indians, the Dade Massacre took place 41 years before Custer's Last Stand and remains a proof of Florida's role as America's wild, wild East.

The Indians attacked "Pilgrimage," burning down one of Moses Levy's sugarhouses and damaging other buildings. The plantation manager had to flee during the attack and the army ordered the rest of the place destroyed to keep it from falling into the hands of the Seminoles. Moses Levy would later seek compensation from Congress only to have the legislative body rule against him.

Levy had spent thousands in developmental costs and legal fees. Was he going to wind up land-poor, unable to help the Jews?

3

The dream of a Jewish homeland, where open worship could be combined with education and a sense of identity, was still firmly in Moses Levy's mind in 1821, when he applied for American citizenship.

He was energized to move ahead on every front and in that year published a plan to establish the first coeducational boarding school for Jewish children in the United States. The school would instruct youngsters in Hebrew and religious matters, as well as "elementary branches of education, useful arts and sciences, as their capacities may warrant."

These arts and sciences were meant to focus on agriculture. It was always an article of faith with Moses Elias Levy that Jews in America should not be like those of Europe, but workers of the land, able to reap fine harvests and be beholden to no one. This was to be the theme of other Jewish settlements subsequently attempted in America and beyond its shores.

He sent the boarding school plan to his friend, Moses Myers, at Norfolk,

Va., to whom he had entrusted his son, David, for education. It was published in a broadside aimed at the American Jewish community, then quite small. The census of 1790 had shown only 2,000 Jews in the country.

Levy acquired some prestigious co-sponsors, including Rabbi M.M. Peixotto of Shearith Israel Congregation, the Sephardic temple in New York City; Mordecai M. Noah, former U.S. consul at Tunis and Judah Zuntz, a prominent Jew in New York.

Rabbi Peixotto's son, Dr. Daniel Peixotto, president of the Medical Society of New York, was also an enthusiast and delivered a speech commending Moses Levy for his "independent stand."

The plan called for buying land "in a healthy and central part of the Union" to establish the scholastic institution. An important condition was that members of its board "must be Israelites." Perhaps Levy's hidden motive was to sell them a piece of his Florida land, but in 1821 Florida could be termed neither healthy nor central.

Certainly the interior of Florida was hardly accessible, except by coastal or riverboat. The territory's few towns were at opposite points on the peninsula. Tallahassee and Jacksonville had not yet been established. Though the Spanish reached the east coast of Florida in 1513 they had not built much more than a few forts and missions. Florida was still as empty as the moon.

Levy's most unusual partner in the school plan was another man who dreamed of establishing a Jewish homeland. He was Mordecai M. Noah, probably the highest-ranking Jewish politician of the day and clearly a Renaissance man. His grandfather and father had been soldiers in the Revolution.

Born in 1735 at Philadelphia, Noah was a newspaper reporter, playwright, lawyer and Tammany Hall politician who served as sheriff, surveyor and city judge in New York. In 1812 Noah was appointed U.S. consul at Tunis. When Noah arranged the freedom of some Americans who were captured and held in Algeria, Secretary of State James Monroe claimed Noah had spent too much money--and worse, freed the wrong men. Monroe wrote that he wanted to remove Noah because his religion was a "barrier" to further effective service in North Africa.

President James Madison upheld Monroe. Noah fought back, published details of the controversy, and gave proof that he had extracted payments from Tunisian leaders which more than covered what he paid Algeria for the release of the Americans. He won a subsequent letter of praise from Madison, but his diplomatic days were over.

In any case, having signed on with Moses Levy on the 1821 boarding school project, Noah was unfazed when it failed for lack of interest.

In 1825 he came out with his own plan to establish a Jewish homeland, to be called Ararat. It was to be located on Grand Island in the Niagara River near Buffalo, N. Y., but it, too, found no underwriters. In 1844, Noah took the homeland idea one step further. He anticipated the Zionist movement by making an appeal to the Christian world to establish Palestine as the Jewish homeland.

Of course, utopian plans of all descriptions--and religious variety-- kept coming up in America. The Am Olam movement attempted 25 separate agrarian settlements for Jews in the U.S. These, too, were predicated on the belief that prejudice against the Jews stemmed from their being commercial middlemen rather than productive workers. One of the Am Olam settlements was Sicily Island in Louisiana. In 1881, 173 men came to the island, cleared 450 acres, built cabins and planted crops. However, the Mississippi flooded and a malaria epidemic followed. Sicily Island was abandoned.

Levy's boarding school plan simply was too ambitious for the times. The first Jewish school of higher learning (Maimonides) wasn't established until 1867 in Philadelphia. It opened with only eight applicants, four of whom didn't show up. In 1873, Hebrew Union College was established at Cincinnati by Rabbi Isaac Mayer Wise, the pioneer of Reform Judaism.

In 1825, Moses Levy went to Europe. He took a residence in Knightsbridge, England, where he engaged in extended correspondence in defense of Jews. Levy was a lifelong confronter of people when it came to defending Judaism.

On his return from England, Levy began to have troubles with his boys. Elias had lasted at Harvard only until 1823, his sophomore year. Young David had been apprenticed to Frederick Myers in 1822 to work in his counting houses. Myers was 'dismayed' to see that David was more interested in reading literature than learning practical business techniques. Both boys evidenced no interest in continuing their father's Judaism. And they were spending a bit too freely.

The family had never been close. As an absentee father, Moses Levy was demanding loyalty without showing much love. In 1827, Levy cut off funds for support of the two boys. All relations were broken off. Moses Levy later claimed that financial reverses due to his litigation made it necessary for him to cut off money to his sons, but his grandson --Wickliffe Yulee--claimed that everything Moses Levy did was cloaked in "sophistic self-reasoning through which he did whatever he wished."

The two boys, without any independent resources, traveled to their father's plantation at Micanopy, where the overseer took them in. The next few years, at least to David, were happy ones in which he said he grew from "heedless boyhood to maturity." The overseer and others on the plantation showed him the ways of the frontier. He was like a kid at camp until 1829 when he took a job as a deputy clerk of the Alachua County Circuit Court.

Perhaps he did so because he was already interested in studying law, or perhaps it was because his father now wanted him to become manager of the Micanopy plantation. At this stage, whatever his father wanted, David hated.

Taking the courthouse job was a fateful move. David was about to step out on his own.

4

For David Levy, the rural delights of Micanopy had been fun. But since taking the clerk's job at the Alachua Circuit Court, he had gotten a glimpse of the powerful world of judges and lawyers. The court was then located at Newnansville, which was the county seat before the establishment of Gainesville. His job at the Circuit Court also dictated occasional trips to St. Augustine, the cultural and political center of east Florida, where the Superior Court was located.

Here young David met Robert Raymond Reid, a lawyer who had come to Florida from Augusta, Georgia. Urbane, versed in literature as well as the law, Reid was to rise to a judgeship, to the presidency of Florida's constitutional convention in 1838-39, and finally to territorial governor. His untimely death from yellow fever in 1841 prevented his playing a more dominant role in the development of Florida. But he was to become teacher and surrogate father, as well as political mentor, to David Levy.

Though his father continued to be a leading citizen of St. Augustine, it was to Reid and not Moses E. Levy that David now turned. After all, his father had cut him off without a dime in 1827.

Instead, David would write to his father, informing him that he intended to study law. Wickliffe Yulee wrote that David fully expected "a life of poverty and obscurity, with no friends or relatives, and with no books or means to acquire them."

This, of course, was melodrama. Judge Reid provided him with a plentiful supply of books, as well as advice and care. By the time David was admitted to the bar in 1832 he was no longer a callow youth but a young bachelor of 22, about five feet, seven inches tall, with a thin face, and Roman nose. He parted his long brown hair on the side and it hung downward in the style of the times.

David was true to his word--for the rest of his life, he took nary a cent from his father. He had learned the law well. Now he began moving into politics under Reid's tutelage.

Florida was not really a two-party state at this time. The first three civilian governors were all Democrats and disciples of Andrew Jackson. But upper Florida had become the area of large plantations. Cotton was booming and the planters became closely allied with three banks. The pro-bank group became the nucleus of the Whig party.

At his entry into politics, David Levy aligned himself with the radical Democrats--as did Reid--who opposed the banks. David was a free trader and a man who defended poor whites who inhabited the outback of the Florida territory.

This, too, was a thumb to the nose at his father, who harbored Whiggish tendencies when it came to matters of finance.

Moses Levy was not entirely accepted by the elite planter class, which consisted of grandees who had migrated southward from Virginia, South Carolina and Georgia, but he WAS that Jewish oddity--a plantation owner and slaveholder.

At the outset, Florida politics had been shaped by Andrew Jackson, the celebrated Indian fighter and war hero who became the territory's first military governor. Oddly enough, the Tennessean never much liked Florida. In 1828, Jackson was elected president. He named a Kentuckian, William Duval, as Florida's first governor. Jackson also had a pair of protégés, succeeding Eaton. Richard Keith Call and John Eaton, who would also play a substantial role in Florida. Unfortunately, Eaton's role would not be glorious.

Eaton had married one Margaret (Peggy) O'Neale Timberlake. She was a "coquettish, impudent girl" who allegedly engaged in what has been euphemistically described as "unpuritanical conduct." Nobody knows if she was actually as bad as her reputation.

She was the scandal of Washington, D.C. but Jackson, who had once resided at her family's boarding house, was Peggy's defender--probably because his own wife, Rachel, had been the object of gossip and snide remarks. Jackson elevated Eaton to a cabinet appointment only to have Peggy's reputation trigger an inter-cabinet fight that threatened to destroy the Jackson administration.

To get Eaton out of Washington, he was appointed Florida's second territorial governor in 1834. He and the infamous Peggy moved to Tallahassee, where Judge Reid would describe him as a "rowdy--his wife drunk or crazy." Reid had admired Gen. Jackson and he was no enemy of Richard Keith Call, but he was disgusted by Eaton and the "noisy senseless crowd" surrounding him in Tallahassee. Call succeeded Eaton as governor, presiding in imperious style but neglecting to erect a political organization to sustain him.

Reid set out to remake Florida politics--and he took two young men with him. They were David Levy and James D. Wescott, both of whom would become Florida's first U.S. Senators in 1845. David started his political journey in 1836 when he was elected to the unicameral Legislative Council of Florida as a representative from St. Johns County. This was the same year Call was appointed governor, succeeding Eaton. In 1837, David Levy was re-elected to the Legislative Council, now a two-chamber body.

Presaging his later role as Florida's chief railroad builder, David Levy introduced a bill incorporating a company which planned to build a railroad at St. Augustine. Moses Elias Levy was one of the proposed incorporators but the company never got off the ground.

In his second legislative term, David Levy reflected Reid's ideas, moving to restrict the functions of banks, particularly the Pensacola Bank in Whig territory. Putting the clamps on banks was to become a central theme of the constitutional convention, which was held in the boomtown of St. Joseph in 1838-39.

Reid would serve as convention president. Levy and Westcott were delegates. St. Joseph was briefly a thriving community, with its own railroad, but it became a ghost town after the cotton boom failed and a yellow fever epidemic struck. The epidemic hit only six years before Dr. John Gorrie of nearby Apalachicola invented his miraculous ice machine and developed a cooling therapy for fever victims.

Moses Elias Levy, who had been angry when David first ran for the Legislative Council, was all but undone when his son became a delegate to the constitutional convention. To him, politics was no place for a Jewish boy.

The constitution was ramrodded through the convention, including language in the 16th article that would allow the legislature to forbid emancipation of slaves or the entry of free blacks, mulattos or persons of color into Florida (language that very nearly barred the admission of Florida to statehood in 1845.)

Reid, Levy et al were successful in ending talk of dividing Florida into two states, east and west Florida. Ever since the 18th century when the British ruled for 20 years, the territory had been called "the Floridas," divided into two entities. Southern partisans thought that by making two states out of Florida they would bolster the strength of pro-slavery states in Congress but realists believed this tactic would antagonize the North and impede statehood.

Reid and his associates were also able to adopt language which sharply restricted the banks, a move that brought them much popularity on the frontier. In particular, they forbade the state from pledging its assets to guarantee bonds issued by the banks.

At the convention, David Levy was to encounter for the first time a charge that was to dog his political career for years--he was accused of being an 'alien.'

That charge was made by Gen. Peter S. Smith, who claimed he did so because David Levy called him an abolitionist on the convention floor. The alien accusation was thinly veiled anti-Semitism and it angered Moses Elias Levy as much as it did his son.

The Whigs in Florida already called people like David Levy "Jacobins" and "Levellers" who "would set the poor against the rich."

The Panic of 1837 had given the Whigs a national political victory but cost them their power in Florida, so an upstart like Levy stuck in their craws. Moreover, his Democratic reforms had hit the banks hard.

The upstart continued to wield power after the convention and by 1839 was among the inner circle of pro-Van Buren Democrats trying to get federal authorities to dump Call from the governorship. Call had split with the new President and moved toward the Whig camp.

A few years earlier, when the Panic of 1837 hit Florida, Call and the legislature had helped bail out the bankers. They had financed the 20-mile-long railroad between Tallahassee and St. Marks, on the Gulf of Mexico. The rail line was used to haul cotton to ships.

Suddenly, the price of cotton plummeted and the banks were in trouble.

Call and the Legislative Council began bailing them out through the issuance of "faith bonds," which pledged territorial assets. These bonds were anathema to the Democrats and David Levy accused the banks of bleeding the public. He swore "unsleeping, undying, eternal enmity to monopoly."

In 1839, David Levy was sent to Washington to push President Van Buren on Call's removal and obtain the president's approval for federal reimbursement to Florida for money paid to voluntary militia who had fought the Seminoles. Levy enlisted Secretary of War Joel Poinsett (the man after whom poinsettias are named) as his principal ally in this effort.

Soon, Reid was named to succeed Call as governor and comforting noises were made about paying for the militia. The soldiers had been paid a princely 20 cents a day if on foot and 60 cents if on horseback.

In 1841, the "Van Burenites" in Florida nominated David Levy to be the territorial delegate to Congress. He promptly denounced the Whigs as the "federal, aristocratic, bank paper, stock-jobbing party."

Now David Levy was playing for big chips. Incumbent Territorial Delegate Charles Downing had lost public favor but was running for re-election. A Whig planter named George T. Ward was also making the race. Charges began to fly against David Levy--he was accused of swindling people for whom he had acted as attorney, of converting to his own use a check made out to Judge Reid, and so on.

David Levy responded that these charges were without foundation "and constitute a fair specimen of the blind malignity with which I am pursued by desperate opponents. "

Finally, Benjamin A. Putnam--a supporter of Downing--pulled the trump slur out of the bag, accusing David of being an "alien." As Peter Smith had done during the St. Joseph convention, Putnam ignored the fact that the second naturalization of Moses Elias Levy had been upheld by the federal courts in 1838.

Instead Putnam claimed Moses Levy's naturalization had taken place 4 1/2 months after David reached the age of 21. By his theory, David was required to file separately for citizenship at 21. Putnam labeled David "an envoy Jew." On other occasions he complained of the bustling industry shown by this "treacherous Jew."

Politics was a hardball game in frontier Florida. David Levy ignored Putnam and blasted Downing as a "truckler in politics ...treacherous and unfaithful in his private and public relations...a secret slanderer and public libeler, and possessed of scarcely honesty enough to elevate him above the common swindler.

In the election of 1841, David Levy received a majority of the votes cast while Downing ran a poor third. Proclaimed Florida's new territorial delegate to Congress, David Levy was about to endure the full fury of politics at the hands of experts in Washington, D.C.

5

On June 21, 1841 David Levy appeared on the floor of the House of Representatives in Washington to present his credentials as the newly elected territorial delegate from Florida. Francis Pickens of South Carolina introduced him. Almost immediately, Rep. Christopher Morgan, a New York Whig, objected on grounds that David Levy was an alien. The Speaker, however, declared Levy qualified. The oath was administered and David Levy took his seat. The alien charge was referred to the Committee on Elections.

The committee was made up of six Whigs and three Democrats--and it did its best to steamroller David Levy. They met when he wasn't present, stalled and postponed. The committee refused to let him submit proofs of citizenship. David pleaded with the House to be heard. After he learned the committee was about to report adversely on his eligibility, he asked for a postponement.

The committee's impending action, he said, would "not only vacate my seat, but, by the sentence of this body, thrust me forth upon the wide world without country, without allegiance or protection, without fellowship in any social compact upon earth."

David Levy had lawyer's arguments, too: Congress had not made citizenship a requisite for a territorial delegate. He said that he met the only specific requirement, that of 12 months prior residence in the country. He pointed out he had been elected to the Florida Legislative Council, which required that he be a citizen; that he had received an advisory opinion from the Attorney General upholding his father's citizenship; that he had obtained a passport; that he had been admitted to the Florida Bar and admitted to practice before the U.S. Court of Appeals, which had also ruled unanimously that his father was a bona fide citizen.

Finally the committee allowed him to present his proofs. On this question of honor, even Moses Elias Levy came forward to testify, despite the feud between them. Florida witnesses spoke about the day Moses Levy entered St. Augustine. The committee reported on March 14, 1842. The report was read, laid on the table and ordered to be printed, but nothing more happened. The House adjourned without further action.

The influence of northern Whigs like former president John Quincy Adams and Joshua R. Giddings, strong abolitionists who had little sympathy with southerners, was felt in the ambiguous House behavior. The Whigs held little love for David Levy and Adams hinted that David Levy, the defender of slavery, himself carried a trace of "African blood."

When the next Congress convened, David Levy's citizenship came up again. This time Rep. J.R. Ingersoll of Pennsylvania produced a memorial from the territory of Florida requesting the issue be settled.

Levy rose to make an angry speech: "When the day comes upon which the solemn and recognized acts of public officers of the government, touching the delicate and inappreciable relation of citizen and country, are brought up after a lapse of twenty-odd years for wanton repudiation by the national representatives, I shall cease--sorrowfully cease--to covet that distinction of American citizenship. When good faith shall depart this government with it will have passed away all that forms the basis of patriotism; all that in verity constitutes the citizen--love and veneration for the institutions, and sympathy with the people of one's country . . ."

He tried to have the alien issue referred to the House Judiciary Committee , but that move failed. Rep. George S. Houston of Alabama got up to argue that by laying the issue on the table without further action, the House had tacitly concurred with David Levy. Once more, the House failed to decide. On May 1, 1844, Rep. E.J. Morris of Pennsylvania moved to refer the matter back to the Committee on Elections. The motion failed and though the subject was mentioned in debate after 1844, it never was resolved in the House.

Parenthetically, David Levy, whose citizenship had been challenged so often, was admitted to practice before the Supreme Court on March 4, 1843.

To Moses Elias Levy the entire episode was an incredible campaign of character assassination. Worse, both his reputation and David's were being trashed at the hands of men serving the national government he cherished. Moses

Levy wrote to the East Florida Herald on Jan. 23, 1843 about the "abuse heaped upon David Levy." He traced the origins of the alien charge back to Peter S. Smith, who he claimed had become "obsessed" with the issue and failed to drop it despite a promise made personally to Moses Levy that he would.

The letter also revealed that Moses Levy was aware that "the people of Florida condemned me for alienating myself from my son when he took the profession of law and, as a consequence, a politician."

So the estranged father was protective of his son's reputation, yet deeply hurt by the venom of the attack and the way the issue was dragged out. His distaste for politics became even stronger.

In 1843, David Levy was re-elected by an even greater majority than in his first race for delegate. He continued fighting for the same issues he had brought with him in 1841--suppression of the Indians, federal compensation for the Florida militia who fought them, as well as for settlers whose property had been destroyed, and--of course--the critical issue of statehood for Florida.

Because he was a man with a voice but no vote in Congress, David Levy had to plead with voting members to carry his views. Like any good salesman, he learned his customers and became highly effective.

Florida's application for statehood had actually been sent to Washington on Feb. 20, 1839, a month after the constitutional convention adjourned. It had been lying fallow for four years. During his first term as a territorial delegate, David Levy hadn't done much to further the application, but in his second term he began a major job of public and Congressional persuasion.

He had obstacles aplenty. The abolitionists opposed entry of a new slave-holding state, but Levy argued that Florida had been made a part of the United States by a solemn treaty--and that an unabrogated treaty was the law of the land.

Meanwhile, to the people of Florida, who were divided on the merits of entering the union, he addressed a "circular letter" soliciting their support for statehood. In the letter, he knocked down the idea of establishing two separate states in the Florida territory as "impracticable at this time."

"If we please to assert the right of self-government, a place in the American Union is ours," he wrote. He also spelled out specific benefits that would accrue to individual Floridians.

Each citizen of the state of Florida would, he said:

1. Acquire the prerogative of self-government.

2. Receive $480 a year for the education of each of his children.

3. Be the beneficiary of federal money for education.

The 16th section of each township would be given to the state or public education. It was estimated that sale of these lands would yield an educational fund of $2.5 million.

The state would also receive 500,000 acres of public land and $400,000 per year for internal improvements. He pointed out these lands would be sufficient to build a railroad from the Atlantic Ocean to the Gulf of Mexico, which would be operated as a public project. The railroad would yield enough profits to defray the cost of the state government, David Levy confidently predicted.

In addition, he argued, Florida would now have a vote in Congress and participate on an equal footing with other states.

"It is now," he added, "at this present juncture, that the South requires to be strengthened, and hereafter our aid will be comparatively valueless. "

Artfully, he stacked up every buzz issue to unite disparate groups in Florida behind him. Roland H. Rerick, in his "Memoirs of Florida," credits this pamphlet as being "one of the most important influences toward securing a strong majority for statehood among the citizens of Florida."

To Florida's small farmers, David Levy asserted that statehood would only cost them $5 to $10 a year in taxes, less than what people were paying in Alabama. After distributing 5,000 copies of his letter, David Levy went to St. Augustine between Congressional sessions in 1844, where he attended a big statehood rally and barbecue.

On Dec. 12, 1844, the Committee on Territories favorably recommended the admission of Florida. Two years of buttonholing by David Levy had paid off--

the stage was set for Florida statehood.

6

When David Levy first reported to Congress, many members grumbled that the U.S. had already had enough of the costly Seminole Wars. President John Tyler, a Virginian who had succeeded William Henry Harrison when that unfortunate man died four months after his inauguration, informed Congress in 1842 that hostilities had ceased. There were only about 80 Seminoles capable of bearing arms in Florida Tyler said. He called further pursuit of these "miserable beings... injudicious and unavailing."

David Levy objected, presenting newspaper articles, letters and even Indian arrows taken from bodies of dead settlers. The situation in Florida, he contented, was vastly different from what the North imagined. Hardly any settler family had escaped loss or injury, and they frequently had to crowd into crude frontier forts to save their lives, he argued. He claimed hostile Indians had cost Florida $8.5 million in actual damages and lost income.

Brandishing an arrow, the delegate told how one Florida man had been killed and his three children set up as targets. They were shot with arrows before their mother's eyes, David Levy said. The mother was then stripped and riddled with seven more arrows. Gravely wounded, she lived long enough to tell the story of the attack. The arrow he displayed came from the body of one of the children, he concluded.

In David Levy's view, President Tyler was caving in to arguments of the Whigs, who were all for cutting off federal spending to fight the Indians in Florida. Indeed, about $20 million had been spent on the Seminole Wars over 6-1/2 years. Tyler, he said, was "a weak man with good impulses but no clearness of principle, and no enlargement of purpose. I cannot express any sympathy with him."

In 1842, the Seminole Wars were declared at an end but in 1855 fighting broke out again in and around Ft. Myers and The Big Cypress Swamp, extending to Sarasota Bay and the Braden plantation in what is now Manatee County. After this last-ditch effort ended in 1858 the handful of remaining Seminoles took refuge in the nearly impenetrable (to whites) Everglades as well as the Big Cypress. Over the years, many more had been shipped west to "Indian territory."

Such antipathy to the Indians rings cruel today, when people are sensitive to the injustices done to native Americans, but to David Levy--and most of Florida--the Seminoles (and the Red Stick Creeks) weren't even native Indians but savage wanderers from Georgia and other points. The Seminoles had absorbed the Creeks, as well as criminals and runaway slaves into their camps, he contended. To Levy, these Indians were "freebooting" and "piratical." The irony is that Levy, who had been falsely accused as an alien, would wage political war on the Seminoles on the grounds that they were hostile "aliens."

In 1842, with the support of Missouri's Sen. Thomas Hart Benton, the Florida delegate won passage for the Armed Occupation Act. This act gave 160 acres of Florida land free to any armed settler who signed up at a federal land office. This was anti-Indian legislation. Yet the boosterism of the era construed it to be a means of bringing peaceful commerce to Florida.

When he went back to campaign for his second term, Levy took this tough stand on Indians to the small farmers and into the camps of trappers and cowboys, who roared their approval. Slave-holding Floridians also supported his views, largely because they looked at Indian warfare as a means of recovering their runaway slaves.

Slavery, of course, was the unresolved undercurrent in every political debate in these years before the war. David Levy proved to be as vigorous a defender of the institution as any public man in the South and clashed many times with his political attackers, the northern Whigs and Free Soilers, on this subject.

Levy drew northern enmity when he tried to amend the 10th article of the Webster-Ashburton treaty with Great Britain, so that seven Florida-bound slaves accused of murdering a man could be returned to the territory to stand trial. The 10th article provided for the return of fugitive criminals from countries party to the treaty. But the British, who had abolished slavery in 1833, refused to consider the criminal charges and declined to surrender the slaves.

David Levy argued that the slaves had escaped from St. Augustine, stolen a boat and reached Cape Florida, where they robbed a house and killed the owner when he tracked them. The slaves then put to sea where a British ship picked them up and took them to Nassau. Levy said they were fugitive criminals within the meaning of the treaty. The British, he charged, were violating the terms of the treaty.

He accused Lord Ashburton of secretly telling New York abolitionists that "friends of the slaves in England would be very watchful to see that no wrong practice took place under the treaty."

Levy was rebutted angrily by Whigs Joshua R. Giddings and by former president John Quincy Adams. Even gag rules of the House failed to curb Giddings' attacks on David Levy. However, the Floridian was able to get a House resolution passed which called for an inquiry into the case. No further action was taken by the House, but this battle solidified David Levy's standing in Florida and stamped him as an unabashed pro-slaver in the North.

The issue that brought David Levy to the peak of his popularity at home was statehood. He had done a thorough job in marshaling support within the territory. Now it was time to persuade Congress.

Among the first objections raised to Florida statehood was directed at the language of the controversial 16th article of the Florida constitution, which empowered the state to prohibit emancipation of slaves, as well as bar entry of freed men, mullatos or persons of color. Levy responded that other southern states had been allowed to adopt their own constitutions as long as they didn't encroach on federal powers. Moreover, he said the people of Florida didn't like to be dictated to. (The slogan on their first state flag read: "Let Us Alone.")

He also denied Florida had insufficient population to qualify for statehood and blamed Indian attacks for an inaccurate census count. One by one, he picked off arguments directed against admission of the slave-holding territory to the union. The pairing of Florida's admission with the free state of Iowa, however, was proposed as a move that would allegedly assure political equilibrium to the nation.

Thus on Feb. 13, 1845, the Florida-Iowa bill passed the House by 154-46 and passed the Senate by 36-9 on March 1.

Florida was now a state--the 27th to join the union, and David Levy had done it! Though he made speeches on the floor, it was his private persuasion, his patrolling the corridors of Congress to buttonhole voting members and what he called his own "manner of accomplishing things" that had done the trick.

As he wrote to James D. Westcott, he had been "laboring like a slave" to get the measure through. But, he claimed his style was low-key. He acted "in quiet demonstration here, and then did it, and succeeded. Never judge me to be inactive because I am silent."

Levy's days as a delegate were about to end. Shortly after Florida was admitted to the union, Territorial Gov. John Branch called a nominating convention to meet in Madison and choose candidates for governor and members of Congress. Branch himself nominated David Levy for the House of Representatives and it was carried by acclamation.

The St. Augustine News of April 26, 1845 issued "a call to arms" to Democrats. "Democrats arouse! Your work is before you--the nominations are made--Florida's favorite son, David Levy, is again candidate. Show your gratitude to the man who faithfully attended your interest..."

The editor added a partisan footnote: "Perhaps the Whiggies would like to know who is David Levy? We pause for a reply."

On May 26, 1845, David Levy was elected to the House over his old enemy, Benjamin Putnam, with a majority of 1100 votes out of 5,000 cast. The Whigs claimed there had been a "corrupt" pre-election arrangement whereby Levy would be chosen by the Florida Legislature as one of the Senators, thus allowing the Democrats to cash in on Levy's name recognition to control the legislature as well as choose two Senators. While Levy denied there was such a deal, the Whig allegations about a Democratic takeover came to pass.

When the legislature voted on June 23, David Levy was a shoo-in for Senator, along with his old political ally, James D. Westcott.

Each won by a 41-16 vote along party lines.

Levy promptly resigned his new seat in the House and William H. Brockenborough was chosen (over Whig Edward C. Cabell) to replace him in a disputed election. The Whig candidate for governor, Richard Keith Call, lost to William D. Moseley.

It was a moment that should have been historic enough--the first man of

Jewish descent elected to the U.S. Senate; a man who was also the parent of Florida statehood. But David Levy had another card to play. On Dec. 26, 1845 he petitioned the Florida Senate to change his name to David Levy Yulee.

According to George R. Fairbanks, the St. Augustine lawyer and confidante of Moses Elias Levy, David Levy had not even known that Yulee had been the family name in Morocco until the lawyer told him. Fairbanks related that: Moses Levy told him that when he came to St. Thomas, "his whole name was Moses Elias Levy Yulee" and that "the name was too long and cumbrous for a business man."

Aware of the fact that there had been no communication between father and son, Fairbanks said he told David what had learned about the name. The name change occurred shortly afterward.

David Levy also explained why he petitioned for a name change. In a letter to the St. Augustine News, he wrote: "The name which my father inherited was that which I asked permission to resume. It was his pleasure to suspend its use after leaving his parental home and employ the name of Levy in its stead. For reasons which will naturally suggest themselves to every heart that holds in proper regard the memory of those through whom we trace our being and lineage, I have thought it becoming in me, as a reverential duty, to reclaim the name and restore it to a place in the register of the human race."

It was also another way to distance himself from his father and the Levy name that had produced such slurs as "little Jew politician."

Certainly few men in American public life have run for office under one name and then sought higher office under a new name. Luckily, Senators were chose by state legislatures and not by popular vote at this time.

At any rate, the Florida Senate read the name-change bill three times on the same day and passed it. The next day the House passed the bill, striking the word "Honorable" preceding his name and unaccountably spelling the last name "Eulee." Final reading was made on Dec. 29 and Gov. William D. Moseley signed the bill on the same day.

David Levy Yulee now had another distinction--the first (and only) man in Florida history to have his name changed by an act of the legislature. His brother Elias, residing in Georgia, also changed his name to Yulee by court action during this period.

At the opening of the 29th Congress, the two new Florida senators were sworn in. They drew lots to determine which would get a full term and Yulee won. On Jan. 12, 1846, Sen. Wescott explained to the Senate that: former Territorial Delegate Levy had changed his name to David Levy Yulee. A resolution was passed allowing him to use the new name.

Because of his prior experience as a territorial delegate, David Levy Yulee was named chairman of the Committee on Private Claims, and a member of the Naval Affairs Committee. There was no Court of Claims in those days so all such claims were settled by acts of Congress.

Though the issue of David Levy Yulee's "alien" status did not reoccur in the Senate, the Pensacola Gazette, a Whig paper, brought it up once more, to no avail.

The new Florida Senator, who was shortly to be labeled the "Florida fire-eater" because of his Calhounist notions on the property rights attached to slavery, immediately set out to win plaudits from the pro-slavery bloc.

He had been in the Senate barely three weeks when he introduced a resolution to annex Cuba to the United States (with the consent of the Cuban inhabitants). This was not just New American expansionism, but a bid to increase slave territory. Importation of slaves to the U.S. had been banned for many years, although continued slave ownership had been upheld. Now here was Yulee proposing, at one fell swoop, to annex an island full of slaves.

He withdrew the resolution five days later, but Whigs were outraged. The Pensacola Gazette expressed "consternation" and said Yulee's proposal was "indelicate, improper and impolite." The Gazette wondered how the Senator "from the youngest state" would dare to do something the "oldest and experienced" senators would not. Yulee, however, was just ahead of his time. Proposals to annex Cuba one way or the other would reoccur for the next 15 years--from other Southerners and on occasion from compliant presidents.

President Polk, who had objected to Yulee's resolution, later tried to purchase Cuba and when the plan leaked out, the New Orleans Bee denounced it as "the unanimate nursling of Mr. Yulee."

Yulee contended that holding Cuba would help the U.S. defend the Gulf.

He also claimed it would yield vast commercial benefits and even spoke to the Charleston Board of Trade on this theme. If this message held appeal to the port of Charleston it had even greater impact in a state 90 miles from Cuba, many of whose residents opposed annexation.

The new Senator had also chafed at being a voteless territorial delegate, but he had been a keen observer of the political process and as a Senator he was to demonstrate great skill as a pork-barrel manipulator, a tradition which Southern politicos have nurtured for better that a century.

But Sen. David Levy Yulee started the practice at a time when states righters opposed taking grants from the federal government. He knew that federal grants of land would translate into state income and yield railroads, bridges and other improvements that could transform the undeveloped Florida wilderness. He obtained more than 1,250,000 acres of federal land for Florida during his Senate tenure, including the Everglades.

7

In 1846, after nearly a year as a U.S. Senator, David Levy Yulee married Nancy Wickliffe, daughter of a former governor of Kentucky and postmaster general in the Tyler administration. He met her at one of the White House balls which Julia Tyler was fond of giving. Washington was a small town in which politics and social life were intertwined.

The fair Nancy was so devout a Presbyterian she was called "the Madonna of the Wickliffe sisters." They were married at the bride's home in Kentucky and honeymooned on a trip through the states that took them to Massachusetts, where they were received by Gov. Winthrop.

The marriage further widened the split between David Levy Yulee and his father. To a career in politics, the name change and marriage, David now added more symbols of alienation. Though he did not formally convert to the Presbyterian Church, he began exhibiting what Prof. Arthur W. Thompson has called "non-sectarian Christianity." This included sometime attendance at church.

One of his daughters, Florida Yulee Neff, told an interviewer in the 1930's that her father did not openly denounce the Jewish faith. Mrs. Neff added that when her father did go to church, "it was an event in the Yulee family."

David's failure to "identify himself actively with the Jewish religion" was the sharpest thrust of all to Moses Elias Levy. In letters that he wrote to Rebecca Gratz in Philadelphia, Moses Levy lamented that "all of my grandchildren are Christians."

In another letter he mused on his fate: "no children, no relations, no nation, nor country and further knowing that God must be present."

Miss Gratz was the recipient of many letters containing Moses Levy's philosophical theories as well as his personal woes. To her he wrote that fulfillment in life could come only through Judaism. In one letter he said that "none but Israelites can do the impossibilities..."

Who was Rebecca Gratz to whom Moses Levy should confess so much of his inner thoughts? The devout daughter of wealthy Sephardic Jews, she was, according to Jacob Rader Marcus, the outstanding Jewish woman in ante-bellum America. Legend has it that she never married because she loved a Gentile who died young. He was the brother of a childhood girlfriend whom Rebecca had nursed during a critical illness.

According to the legend her devotion to the sick friend and her own loss of love were evidence of a selflessness that profoundly impressed American author and diplomat Washington Irving, who told the tale to Sir Walter Scott. Scott then incorporated it into his novel "Ivanhoe," with Rebecca Gratz serving as the model for the book's Rebecca.

Be that as it may, Rebecca Gratz probably knew Moses Elias Levy through her work in founding the first Jewish Sunday school in America, which she established in 1838. She knew of Levy's prior effort to establish a Jewish school. He in turn knew of her many good works and was acquainted with her father, one of the most successful Jewish businessmen in the country.

Levy admired her piety, sometimes feeling that he had lost his earlier goal of living a life of religious purpose. He wrote Rebecca: "to love God, you have to contemplate his works and fix your mind on the act you are doing, acknowledging in mind that all the power to do the act comes from him. By contemplating in detail the surroundings of the act you can have God in these his works and mercies. This love begets concentration and equilibrium. Equilibrium obtained, man is restored. This Israel alone can do, because they alone have had the will of God revealed to them..."

Many years later when David Levy Yulee was administering his father's estate, he wrote a lengthy document which dealt in part with his father's religious zeal. He put the primary blame for their split on his father's theological bent. A thaw in their relations occurred with the birth of David's first child. A reconciliation took place shortly afterward that lasted until Moses Elias Levy died on Sept. 7, 1854 while visiting a spa in Virginia.

In this memoir, David Levy Yulee stated the "Causes of our separation were similar to those which had previously separated him from his wife, his older son and to more or less an extent, from his daughters, modified in this case by the dependence of their sex. The peculiar views and conditions of mind of this excellent man, which thus wrecked the unity of his family, was well understood among its members. I threw a veil over them."

Yulee also said his father's affection for his wife, Nancy, grew pronounced after he and his father reconciled. Moses Levy wrote here many notes containing phrases like "my loved one" and "daughter of my soul." Once, after hearing her at the piano, Moses Levy wrote a note that concluded, "Farewell, faithful mirror of my affections and mind."

Before he died Moses Levy was to write: "I say again in justice, cut not off from your heart your child, nor aught springing from you, from religious differences..."

The Yulee children, Wickliffe, Florida, Margaret and Nanny Christian were brought up as Christians. This was often true of children born of inter-marriage. According to Malcolm H. Stern, only eight percent of ante-bellum marriages between Jews and Christians resulted in conversion. More often than not, the Christian marriage partner was female and the children followed her faith.

As the oldest child, Wickliffe was most sharply aware of the conflict between his father and grandfather. When he wrote about it after the turn of the century, he did so in language that was not kind to Moses Elias Levy. He portrayed his grandfather as a fanatic in all he did, who harbored strange notions on economics as well as religion.

Nancy Wickliffe Yulee, of course, has been born to the purple. The family estate near Bardstown, Ky. was large and there were many slaves. Her father had been a governor of his state and a cabinet officer, so she was used to high social circles. She moved within these circles comfortably.

In Florida she was a social celebrity talked about at the same level as Kate Willis Gray Murat, the grand niece of George Washington who married Napoleon's nephew, Achille Murat. Murat declined to be called "Prince Murat." He was a tobacco-chewing type with decidedly unroyal habits such as an aversion to changing clothes. (The Murats once bought a home from Moses Elias Levy called "Parthenope," at the junction of the Matanzas River and Moses Creek in east Florida. Later they lived at Lipona, their plantation eight miles from Tallahassee.)

After the Civil War, the widowed Kate Murat was so destitute her former slaves offered her food. Mrs. Yulee, despite grievous personal property losses, fared much better. Though she had accepted slavery as much as her husband, she cared for their future after the war ended, writing to her husband while he was in prison on June 20, 1865: "The Negroes are not doing very well, but I will be patient, for I want to do them good. They will take some time to settle in their new condition."

Mrs. Yulee was a Florida regent of the Mount Vernon Ladies Association, which bought George Washington's home on the banks of the Potomac and preserved it. In 1876, long after her husband had left politics, Mrs. Yulee declined an invitation to be a Florida delegate to the U.S. Centennial celebration held in Philadelphia. Gov. Harrison Reed then appointed Ellen Call Long, the oldest daughter of Richard Keith Call.

Because home entertainment played so large a role in 19th century life, Mrs. Yulee was also noted for presiding over several fine mansions in Florida as well as homes in Washington, D.C. She once turned "Marguerita," her home a Homosassa into a shelter for healthy children during a scarlet fever epidemic.

She patiently supported her workaholic husband with few complaints and threw herself into the role of Senate wife with marked success, so that throughout their Washington days the Yulees were regarded highly in social circles where political slurs often had little effect.

8

The paradox of Sen. David Levy Yulee was that he had gone to Washington expounding populism, attacking the economic policies of the planter class. Yet he subscribed to the social customs set by this elite group. Prior to the Civil War, he expanded his own plantation and slave holdings. His pride was his sugar plantation at Homosassa, which at one time had 100 slaves.

His views on slavery and states' rights were patterned on those of Sen. John C. Calhoun of South Carolina, the man who had fostered the doctrine of nullification only to be beaten by Andrew Jackson, an all-out defender of the union.

South Carolinians like Calhoun were the most passionate of the secessionists and many of them settled in Florida. In the 1840's, David Levy Yulee was a staunch defender of Southern ways. It was a time of territorial expansion--more than a million square miles of new territory had come under U.S. control as a result of annexation of Texas, settlement of the dispute over Oregon and defeat of Mexico.

Thus the raging debate was whether these new territories would be slave or free. Under Yulee's reasoning, it was unconstitutional to abridge the right of any slaveholder to bring his "property" into any territory. The opponents just as heatedly contended Congress could prohibit slavery in the territories.

In 1846, when Rep. David Wilmot of Pennsylvania introduced an amendment to prohibit introduction of slavery in land acquired from Mexico under the treaty of Guadeloupe Hidalgo, Yulee had been in the front ranks of the opponents. The southerners in the Senate won that skirmish and the Wilmot Proviso failed. The discovery of gold in California in 1848 re-focused the slavery debate anew as the nation hastened to grant statehood to this rich territory.

By 1849, when statehood for California seemed imminent, Yulee opposed its admission as a free state. He wrote to Calhoun when Congress adjourned in March, predicting that California would be the South's chief problem in the next session. He said that other issues would include emancipation of slaves in the District of Columbia, interstate slave trade and annexation of Canada. He missed on Canada but was right about the others.

From this point on, David Levy Yulee beat the drum for state sovereignty. He came out in favor of holding a southern convention to decide the California issue (he wanted to divide the state into separate free and slaveholding sections). He also wanted the convention to talk about organizing a "States' right Republican party." If all remedies failed, Yulee said, "the inevitable alternative is an amendment of the compact of the union or its dissolution."

He hoped to amend the Constitution, but if the Constitution couldn't be amended, Yulee said, "I think the truest and best policy is to take steps at once for separation...we must have fireside and peace...we must hold and enjoy our customs and property in tranquility."

Hard lines were being drawn at the close of 1849, Meanwhile, Sen. Westcott, Yulee's old ally in Florida, gave notice on March 4 that he wouldn't run for re-election. The Florida Legislature replaced him with Jackson Morton, an ex-Virginian and Whig.

In August of 1850 Yulee spoke for four hours (over three days) to block Henry Clay's proposal on admission of California. Clay, the Kentuckian whose compromises in 1820 and 1833 held the country together, had come back to the Senate after eight years absence to offer his greatest package, the Compromise of 1850.

It was actually six resolutions packaged in five bills: admission of California as a free state; creation of the territories of New Mexico and Utah without restriction as to slavery; assumption of the debt of Texas which had been contracted prior to annexation and relinquishment of Texas' claim to eastern New Mexico; prohibition of slavery in Washington, D.C.; the Fugitive Slave Act, to provide more effective return of slaves to their masters, and the assertion that Congress could not forbid existing interstate slave trade.

In addition to opposing entry of free California, Yulee took the floor to amend the New Mexico-Utah bill. He wanted to assure slave owners protection as long as New Mexico and Utah remained territories. The move failed. As to

California, Yulee and his new colleague, Sen. Morton, were among 10 Southerners who voted against admission.

The compromise was signed into law by a new president, Millard Fillmore, Zachary Taylor having died on July 9 after becoming ill at dedicatory ceremonies for the Washington Monument.

Yulee felt he was being "forced down into a pot and the lid clamped on," but his career was about to be rudely interrupted by a reversal of local political fortune. He had come to Washington in 1841 when the Whigs won the presidency but lost Florida. Now David Levy Yulee was to feel the Whig's revenge in that party's last fling before disappearing.

Florida Whigs had supported the Compromise of 1850. Many were thorough unionists who had no stomach for secession, among them former Territorial Gov. Richard Keith Call and the Whig nominee for Congress, Edward Cabell, who had made an unsuccessful try for the House in 1845. In 1850, Cabell came out strongly for the union, beating Maj. John Beard, a former North Carolinian who was rabidly for secession.

The Florida Legislature met in November, but curiously did nothing about electing two Senators. Instead it met on Jan. 13 and Yulee's name was placed in nomination without opposition. On the first ballot, 29 votes were cast for Yulee and 29 were returned blank. The chair ruled no election and a second ballot was ordered. No change. On the third vote, Yulee received 28 votes and 30 others were blank. The assembly then adjourned.

Two days later, Stephen E. Mallory of Key West was nominated. Mallory was a Democrat and had been a Yulee supporter. A coalition of Whigs and disaffected South Florida Democrats combined to nominate Mallory without his foreknowledge or consent. On the fourth ballot, Mallory received 31 votes and Yulee 23, four members casting blank ballots. Mallory was elected. Twenty-four Whigs and seven Democrats had combined to take the Senate seat away from Yulee.

It wasn't just national political issues that had toppled Yulee, though he opposed most of the Compromise of 1850. The Democrats from South Florida didn't like the plans for a cross-state railroad which he had been pursuing since Florida's entry into the union. They were opposed to Yulee's proposed ports at Fernandina and Cedar Key because they would draw business away from an established port in Key West. The Whigs, of course, had detested Yulee since his entry into state politics.

Who was Mallory? The son of a sea captain from Connecticut and an Irish immigrant mother, he had been born on Trinidad in 1813. When his father died his mother began running a boarding house at Key West. Mallory was to become the collector of customs, a maritime correspondent for a New York newspaper, a lawyer and eventually a county judge. The Whigs liked the fact that Mallory had no sympathy for secession. There was little overt opposition to the fact that he was a Catholic.

Yulee's unexpected defeat went down hard. On March 8, 1851 he gave notice in Congress that he intended to contest the election. He contended he was the only nominee to receive more than a majority of a quorum on the first ballot. Further, he argued that no votes had been cast for any other person on the first ballot. Therefore, Mallory's election was invalid, Yulee claimed.

Returning to his Homosassa mansion, "Marguerita," Yulee was feted by Democrats from central Florida, to whom he reiterated his refusal to bow to northern power and his continued defense of slavery as private property.

Mallory was sworn in and was named to Yulee's former seat on the Committee on Naval Affairs. Assorted southern Senators made attempts to block Mallory's entry to the upper body, but Henry Clay objected on the grounds that Mallory held a valid certificate of election from the state of Florida.

Meanwhile, Yulee hired two of the top lawyers in the country to argue his case, Reverdy Johnson and Edwin M. Stanton (the very same Stanton, who, as Lincoln's Secretary of War, was to disregard any friendship for Yulee and approve his imprisonment on a trumped-up charge of treason.) Despite this high-powered legal representation, Mallory's election was upheld on Aug. 28, 1852. The Senate committee commented that Yulee should have made his challenge in the Florida Legislature when the presiding officer ruled no election.

Yulee spoke in his own defense for two hours but the Senate voted 41-0 to confirm Mallory's election. After a decade of Washington service, Yulee was out of public office.

Yulee bore no personal grudge against Mallory and four years later he was returned to the Senate, succeeding Jackson Morton. Yulee was not at rest, however.

He went home to fulfill the railroad development dreams which he had been pursuing since 1841.

9

David Levy Yulee's celebrated industry in snaring federal dollars for state improvements actually began when he was a territorial delegate. In his first term as a non-voting delegate, he won a $271,708 appropriation for improving the naval yards in Florida, $20,000 to complete the state capitol building at Tallahassee and $3,000 to prepare a cost estimate for a survey of railroad route to connect the Atlantic and Gulf coasts.

At the time he was thinking of the cross-state railroad as a public enterprise. This was in line with what he later advocated in his "circular letter" that shaped Florida public opinion to support statehood.

The first railroad charter in the state had been granted by the Florida Territorial Legislative Council in 1835, for a line from the St. Johns River to St. Augustine. When the council, with David Levy serving, passed another act in 1833 to incorporate the road, his father was one of the proposed incorporators. The St. Augustine line did not go forward, however.

In 1836, Congress approved funds for a survey of a cross-state canal, which came to naught. The predominant interest in Florida was in building railroads. The St. Joseph & Wimico Railroad provided a short rail line to the Apalachicola River in 1836. In 1837, the 20-mile line from Tallahassee to St. Marks was built. Both of these early lines got cotton to market and as a result, rail was being looked at as essential to Florida's development.

The Yulee railroad plan claimed to have staked out the shortest and most direct route across Florida. It would run from Fernandina on the Atlantic Ocean to Cedar Key on the Gulf of Mexico. Cedar Key had been discovered in 1834 by men looking for cedar trees. Fernandina was on Amelia Island, just across the St. Mary's river from Georgia. It had been used as a port by the Spanish and was home to smugglers, illegal slave runners and adventurers prior to U.S. acquisition.

"...Such a road ought to be, and I hope it will be, the property of the state," David Levy had stated in his pre-statehood circular letter. But this never happened because the proposed railroad became embroiled in partisan politics. A charter was issued for a cross-state railroad in 1849 (the Atlantic and Gulf Railroad) only to expire before any work was done.

Whig Governor Thomas Brown blocked David Levy Yulee's attempt to capitalize the Atlantic and Gulf because the Whigs preferred a Jacksonville to Pensacola route. Denied state cooperation as long as the Whigs were in charge, Yulee shifted his approach.

Not until June 8, 1853, when Yulee was no longer a member of the

Senate, was a state charter obtained for the Florida Railroad Company, as it was now known. It was incorporated as a private company with a capitalization of $1 million and Yulee was elected its first president.

However, Yulee angered Democrats from Key West, who thought the railroad terminus at Cedar Key would snatch shipping business from their established port. A subsequent alliance of south Florida Democrats and Whigs had cost Yulee his Senate seat in 1850.

The mid-Florida town of Tampa also started pushing for the west coast terminus. Yulee tried to beat down the idea, claiming Tampa Bay was too shallow for port use. Besides, he added, Cedar Key was closer to New Orleans.

In 1855 Tampa and Cedar Key were made dual West Coast terminals by the Florida Legislature. (Actually, Tampa was made the terminus with "an extension to Cedar Key.")

About this time, Yulee also became a backer of another ambitious southern plan, the Tehuantepec Railroad, which many in the South saw as a means of opening up commerce to the Pacific Coast. The proposed railroad was to cross the Tehuantepec isthmus of northwest Mexico and connect New Orleans to the Pacific. The line through Mexico would open the cotton and agricultural products of the Mississippi valley to Europe as well as the far west. Yulee saw a ready transportation link between Cedar Key and New Orleans.

Judah P. Benjamin, of Louisiana, went to Mexico to negotiate for right-of-way but this plan also failed. Though the South would ultimately need a rail line to the west coast it never got one when it needed it during the Civil War.

Primarily, entrepreneur David Levy Yulee concentrated his attention on making the Florida railroad a reality. He bought Fernandina and almost all of Amelia Island for less than $9,000, and acquired other properties pertinent to the railroad. Though he was out of the Senate, he traded on his political know-how to lobby for federal aid, winning support from his old Senate colleague, Sen. Augustus Dodge of Iowa, as well as Florida Congressman August Maxwell.

In 1854, Yulee, along with James T. Archer, Richard A. Long, Dr. Abel S. Baldwin and John C. Pelot, was named by the governor to draw up a plan for handling railroads and canals as internal improvements in the state. Yulee fathered the plan, which was implemented by an 1855 act. Former federal swamp and overflow lands which had been held by a state board were now placed under a reorganized trust, to be run by the governor and cabinet. This landmark act established the Internal Improvement Fund (IIF), an entity that functions to this day.

Having Yulee and Baldwin on the same board must have been interesting. Baldwin was president of the Florida, Atlantic and Gulf Central, which had Jacksonville as its eastern terminus on a 60-mile line to Alligator (Lake City).

The IIF was empowered to approve any railroad plans which traversed the lands held in trust. Railroads already chartered were required to give the IIF trustees notice of their acceptance of terms of the act within six months.

The panel recommended a system of railroads which would connect

Fernandina to Tampa, Jacksonville to Pensacola and improvements to existing line like the Tallahassee-St. Marks, as well as a St. Johns-Indian River canal.

Meanwhile, a Democratic governor, James E. Broome, replaced Whig Thomas Brown, who had been a thorn in Yulee's side. The Florida Legislature followed up by voting to send Yulee back to the Senate in December of 1854, restoring him to political power.

On Jan. 17, 1855 a contract was let to a man named Anson Bangs to start construction of the railroad. However, the contract was cancelled on June 11. Another contract was let--this time to Joseph Finnegan & Co. Finnegan and his partner, A.H. Cole, had a third partner, Alexander McRae, of Wilmington, N.C. McRae had built rail lines in the Carolinas and would serve as chief engineer of the Florida Railroad.

Crews went to work during the winter of 1855-56. Having notified the IIF that the railroad accepted terms of the act, Yulee and his stockholders held their first meeting on March 3,1855 in Jacksonville.

David Levy Yulee, once a youthful thunderer against entrenched economic interest, now acted like a captain of industry. He lobbied to block a railroad between Pensacola and Savannah and was critical of any competing line that crossed into Georgia. The head of steam he had generated as a railroad builder was unquenchable.

Yulee carried his railroad cap with him when he went back to the U.S. Senate for a second term, succeeding his former colleague, Jackson Morton. He was undaunted by the prospect of trying to build a railroad while simultaneously serving in the Senate, though he would later complain about the task being too much for one man.

By 1856, Yulee got Congress to approve substantial land grants for his expanded railroad as well as for two proposed lines, one between Jacksonville and Pensacola and another from Pensacola to Alabama. These grants facilitated future land development as well because they extended six miles deep on either side of the right-of-way. In addition, the bill authorized transportation of mail on these lines. Yulee's Florida Railroad got close to 500,000 acres of federal land via these grants.

Work on the railroad moved briskly despite the hazards of the terrain. Yulee bought his rails in England because there was no foundry in the South capable of making them. The spikes came from Baltimore, Md. and Richmond, Va. Yulee also hired Edwin M. Stanton as the railroad's bond attorney.

The railroad issued bonds backed by mortgages on the town property which the railroad owned at Fernandina (quite an increase over the purchase price of $9,000.) Cedar Key property was worth $750,000. Riggs & Co. of Washington, D.C. distributed $250,000 worth of these bonds in a single month.

Another financial panic hit in 1857 and by 1859 Yulee had to borrow $35,000 from August Belmont & Co. in New York, Riggs & Co. in Washington, and from James Soutter, president of the Bank of the Republic, to pay interest on the outstanding bonds.

To obtain the money, Yulee mortgaged 80 of his slaves at his Homosassa sugar plantation as well as some railroad property. As financial conditions worsened, Yulee struggled on. Finnegan & Co. was having difficulty in buying construction materials without ready cash.

Yulee was able to save the railroad by persuading northern investors to increase their holdings. Acquiring $224,000 in bonds and 7,434 shares of stock, the northern investors now paid Finnegan's construction bills. Railroad construction was mostly done by slave labor, some of who were hired from their owners in North Carolina and Virginia at the rate of $20 per month for adults and $8 for boys. Some Irish immigrant labor was used, too.

Yulee never blinked when, as a sitting senator, he arranged public policies to benefit his own interests. But this was a nationwide phenomenon. Entrepreneurs all over America were doing the same thing. Historian Daniel Boorstin notes that William B. Ogden, the Chicago mayor and railroad builder, did much the same thing.

"He could not forget that everything which benefitted Chicago, or built up the great West, benefitted him..." Boorstin wrote.

And so it was with David Yulee. People like transportation writer Henry V. Poor touted the Florida Railroad as being as significant an advance as the Erie Canal. De Bow's Review in New Orleans said Yulee's road was "destined to be one of the most important in the country."

Yulee worked obsessively and his wife wrote to complain that the railroad was "becoming my enemy" by threatening her husband's health. Political problems followed on the heels of financial troubles.

Gov. Madison S. Perry turned up in Fernandina one day and told Yulee the railroad had to be routed via Micanopy to Cedar Key, rather than through Gainesville, a route which had already been approved and was under construction.

Perry owned a plantation in Micanopy. Perry threatened Yulee to the point that the Senator cried, "Go ahead, do your worst!" Later Yulee was to tell the governor he couldn't dictate the policies of the Florida Railroad nor change routes that already had been approved by the U.S. and the IIF.

Perry then tried to stop construction and informed the legislature of alleged engineering irregularities, enlisting a disgruntled former railroad construction engineer named Alfred Sears to testify.

The Legislature appointed a select committee to look into the allegations, but Yulee and State Sen. George W. Call objected. A Democrat and nephew of Richard Keith Call, George Call was secretary of the railroad. They said Sears' complaints were about superficial matters.

Next, Perry complained that Cedar Key harbor was too shallow to admit steamers as required by state charter. Yulee had to produce a Lt. Berryman of the U.S. Coastal Survey to attest that the harbor was indeed deep enough. On Jan. 10, 1859, the Florida select committee cleared the Florida Railroad of Sears' charges.

Sen. Yulee, meanwhile had obtained a $500,000 contract for tri-weekly mail service by rail and boat from New York to New Orleans. As chairman of the

Senate Post Office Committee, he also authorized a new mail route between Cedar Key and Havana. His brother-in-law, Joseph Holt, coincidentally was Postmaster General at the time and just happened to own a lot in Fernandina.

Daily steamboat service from Charleston to Fernandina began in 1859 and by 1860 telegraph service was operational at Fernandina to northern and western points. The first message sent was to the New York Chamber of Commerce touting the new port.

Yulee now obtained yet another charter from the Florida Legislature. This one authorized the Florida Peninsula Railroad, which would pass down the west coast of the state, through Ocala and thence to Tampa, bypassing Micanopy, but keeping its leg to Cedar Key. Yulee was elected president of the Florida Peninsula Railroad.

Coincidentally, Tampa boosters put together at this time a proposed bond subscription of $1 million for a plan called the Honduras Railroad Co. Briefly, passengers would board a ship in Tampa (after leaving Yulee's train) and sail to Honduras, where a new railroad line would take them across a narrow part of the isthmus to the Pacific. Here they would board another vessel to California.

It was a venturesome idea, anticipating the Panama Canal by many years. If it had worked, it would have linked Florida and California by a complex rail and steamboat arrangement. But the Honduras Railroad failed for lack of adequate financing.

If the Honduras bubble had burst, it was not a serious impediment to

Yulee, who declared his chief ambition was to see his original 155-mile rail line built, "every mile of it--and not until then will I regard myself 'off duty'."

The first train from Fernandina reached Baldwin on Sept. 11, 1857. By April 21, 1859 service reached Gainesville. On June 12, 1860, the original Fernandina to Cedar Key route was completed. Trustees of the IIF were informed on May 28 that 155.5 miles were complete. At the time, the rolling stock consisted of two locomotives, two passenger cars, one mail/baggage car, two stock cars, eight boxcars and 35 platform cars.

When the line was completed in 1860 the press was lavish in its praise--no other man in the state, the papers said, could have completed "the great enterprise." David Levy Yulee, once more, was described as "untiring and indefatigable, his energy knows no flagging."

10

Senator Yulee had returned to Congress during increasingly bitter days. His colleague, Stephen Mallory, was the man who had taken his Senate seat away in 1850. Yet the two men were to become a team in national politics. By the time secession was inevitable Yulee--the onetime "fire-eater"--and Mallory, who had never wanted secession, were exceptions to the fever that gripped most Senators from the deep South.

Mallory had taken over Yulee's former chairmanship of the Senate Committee on Naval Affairs, gaining an expertise that would serve him well as Confederate Secretary of the Navy, 1861-65. During that term Mallory would actually implement an idea that had originated in Yulee's term on the committee-- the building of ironclad ships, which revolutionized naval warfare.

Though Florida's economy relied in part on provision of timber and "naval stores" for wooden vessels, iron hulls were deemed by both senators to be the vessels of the future. Not only were they immune to shelling in battle, but their resistance to rot and teredos (marine worms) insured long use. Yulee urged appropriations for iron ships and was responsible for getting funds to strengthen federal forts at Pensacola.

Mallory, who regarded secession as the equivalent of revolution, became the Confederacy's only cabinet member to serve from beginning to end. Although he was a Catholic, Mallory was accused by the northern press of being a Jew. The same charge was hurled against the Confederate minister to France, John Slidell, whose daughter married a Jewish banker in France.

Strangely enough, it was Yulee's fate as chairman of the naval affairs committee to clash with Commodore Uriah P. Levy, a hero of the War of 1812 and the only Jew to rise to command in the pre-Civil War Navy. Because of anti-Semitism, Commodore Levy was court-martialed six times and thrown out of the Navy twice but repeatedly fought all charges and won reinstatement. Uriah Levy was no relation to David Levy Yulee but in his stubborn defense of Judaism, he was very much like Yulee's father, Moses Elias Levy.

Uriah Levy ran away to sea as a child and became a ship's master as a teenager. When insulted because of his religion, he fought a duel and killed a man. Throughout his career in the Navy, he battled anti-Semitism with the same ferocity he displayed in opposing flogging.

The commodore even wanted his tombstone engraved to give him credit for ending flogging. He was court-martialed for putting bird's feathers and tar on a seaman's behind rather than flog the man. It took a celebrated trial and presidential decree to reinstate Commodore Levy in the Navy. His views also brought him before Sen. Yulee, who held hearings and openly supported flogging.

When Sen. John P. Hale, an abolitionist from New Hampshire, introduced a bill to abolish flogging, Yulee opposed it, accepting the Navy's view that it was the only effective means of maintaining discipline on board ship. Flogging was curbed in 1850 but not actually abolished till the Civil War.

As chairman of the naval affairs committee, Yulee also initiated a move to pay Stephen Decatur and his men $100,000 for services in the War of 1812--a sum to be treated as "prize money" for the recapture and burning of the ship Philadelphia while it was in the hands of Tripoli. If it had passed (it failed by two votes), the measure would have accomplished what Congress failed to do more than 40 years earlier.

In his second term, Yulee took chairmanship of the Committee on the Post Office & Post Roads, where he presided over a bill to abolish the Congressional franking privilege and increase postal rates. The committee--in typical Congressional wisdom--voted to raise the rates but instead of abolishing the frank, they adopted an amendment to reimburse the Post Office for carrying franked mail!

Yulee introduced a resolution in January, 1860, to permit the Post Office to transmit "money and valuable packets," thus prescribing a plan for postal money orders which was finally begun in 1864, after Yulee had left the Senate. In 1859, Yulee's brother-in-law, Joseph Holt, was appointed Postmaster General. The hardheaded Hold and Yulee began to have differences.

Hold didn't want Congressional interference in the way he supervised the postal service. He tried to cut out stagecoach mail service to California, and terminated mail service down the Mississippi as well as between Charleston and Key West, making Yulee and other southerners angry. Later, Holt became President Buchanan's Secretary of War, clashing once again--and more fatefully--with Yulee.

Meanwhile, during four years out of the Senate, Yulee had not ignored political life, though he had concentrated on his railroad. He had gone to the Democratic National Convention, held in Baltimore in 1852, and headed the Florida delegation. The convention nominated for president Franklin Pierce, a New Hampshire man with pro-South attitudes. Yulee accepted Pierce but really was a backer of Sen. Stephen A. Douglas of Illinois, whom he also supported in 1856 and reluctantly quit in 1860.

Douglas had expounded a theory in letting local sovereignty settle the slave issue in territories. Yulee had served with Douglas in both houses of Congress and admired him. (Douglas was a railroad booster, too.) Yulee had long maintained that sovereignty resided exclusively in the people of the states. He claimed that it was unconstitutional to abridge the right of slaveholders to take their property into any territory. In Douglas, he saw an electable northerner who would preserve southern rights. He stuck with Douglas until the Illinois Senator reversed himself and declared a territory could bar slavery by denying it police protection. That tore things.

"I shall vote for Breckinridge," Yulee wrote just before the election of 1860. John C. Breckenridge of Kentucky, the former vice president, had been persuaded by southerners to run. Along with John Bell, the Constitutional Union Party candidate, and Douglas, they succeeded in splitting the vote so that Lincoln won with less than a majority of the popular vote. Between them the three candidates polled 900,000 more votes than Lincoln.

Passage of the Kansas-Nebraska Act in 1854 (before Yulee returned to the Senate) had triggered the rise of a new party, the Republicans. The Whigs were passing out of existence. The Republicans--and Yulee opposed their use of the name--were a coalition of "Conscience Whigs," abolitionists and Free Soilers. New York editor Horace Greeley claimed to have given them the name of Republicans. As far as most southerners were concerned, Yulee included, it would be intolerable if the "black" Republicans ever got control of the federal government and stopped extension of slavery into the territories.

In 1856, the Republicans came up with Gen. John C. Fremont as presidential nominee. Called "The Pathfinder" because of his western explorations, he gave James Buchanan a close but losing race for the presidency. Even though Fremont's father-in-law was the pro-South Senator Thomas Hart Benton of Missouri, Fremont was an abolitionist who was anathema to the South. (During the Civil War, Gen. Fremont issued an emancipation proclamation as commander of union troops in the West, infuriating Lincoln, whom he had failed to consult.)

When the Whigs collapsed they gave impetus to yet another phenomenon, the American or Know-Nothing party. Many ex-Florida Whigs including R.K. Call shifted to the Know Nothings, who nominated his cousin, David S. Walker, for Florida governor in 1856. A member of the IIF board, Walker lost the governorship in a tough race with Madison S. Perry, a "secesh" radical born in South Carolina.

Yulee had no love for the Know Nothings, who were anti-foreigner, anti-Catholic nativists. They were to campaign against the "Jew dynasty" in Florida, meaning Yulee and his organization. Yulee was once again denounced as an "alien, traitor and proselyte."

Yet, Oddly enough, there were some Jews who supported the Know Nothings despite their anti-foreigner rhetoric. The Know Nothings elected a Jewish man, Lewis C. Levin of Philadelphia, to Congress. And in 1854, their nominee for governor of New York was a Jew named Daniel Ullman. Nevertheless, most Jews in the South had no taste for this party or its prejudice, according to historian Bertram W. Korn.

The Know Nothings had actually been founded in 1849 as a secret order (whose members' response to questions was: "I know nothing"). It rose briefly to some standing, but it became so split by the slavery issue that the party broke up. At times the party seemed blind to Jews, focusing instead on Catholic Irish and German immigrants who, it was feared, would overwhelm American institutions.

The schizophrenia rampant at this time kept building. Yulee, who had once contended that secession was the South's "great preservative right," had become more moderate by 1860, reluctant to get out of the union. Even if Lincoln was elected, he preferred the peaceful departure of Florida from the union, with a right to return. Gov. Perry and the separatists who had control of the state, however, clamored for secession without any ifs or buts. Yet Yulee was a pragmatic politician, capable of speaking out of both sides of his mouth.

During the five months between the presidential election of 1860 and the start of the Civil War, he supported some but not all secessionist strategies in Congress; voted for resolutions on slavery that Jefferson Davis introduced, but refused to sign a southern manifesto drafted by Rep. James L. Pugh of Alabama and Sen. Louis Wigfall of Texas. Nor was he keen to attack Ft. Pickens at Pensacola or Ft. Sumter in South Carolina. Yet, he busied himself gathering information that would be useful to the South, such as names of Floridians in the U.S. military.

The war could just as well have started in Florida. Three months before Ft. Sumter, President Buchanan was persuaded by Yulee's brother-in-law, Joseph Holt, to reinforce the federal forts at Pensacola and destroy the arsenal at Chattahoochee. Buchanan, however, was reluctant to take any step that would be provocative.

While Buchanan's timidity and unwillingness to reinforce Ft. Sumter led it to fall in April, it was Florida's reluctance to attack Ft. Pickens when it was only lightly defended in January that kept open warfare against a union bastion delayed for three months.

The arsenal wasn't destroyed and was seized by Florida militia just prior to secession. Ft. Marion in St. Augustine, guarded by one man, also fell to Florida militia. The militia never tackled the forts at Pensacola and Key West, which the union held throughout the war. An uneasy truce of sorts held at Ft. Pickens, largely because Sens. Yulee and Mallory were able to persuade Buchanan not to implement Holt's recommendations.

Yulee had learned of Holt's plans either in late December, 1860 or early in January of 1861. The moderate Yulee abruptly lost control. He wrote to Gen. Joseph Finnegan, commander of Florida troops, urging him to seek immediate occupation of all federal forts, naval stations and arsenals in Florida. Such an action was precisely what Gov. Perry desired. Yulee also unwisely wrote "I shall give the enemy another shot before retiring. I say enemy. Yes, I am theirs and they are mine; I am willing to be their masters but not their brothers."

The letter to Finnegan infuriated Holt, with whom relations were already strained, and after the war it became the basis for Yulee's imprisonment at Holt's angry insistence. Yulee was to claim that his bellicose letter was due to a "special momentary excitement." Florida historian Dorothy Dodd nonetheless characterized it as "an entirely gratuitous blessing on the secession movement." After the war he made an attempt to deny the episode.

Yulee's son contended his father's "economic interests" made him averse to secession, although the N.Y. Times charged that "the railroad class" wanted secession so as to unload heavy debts to northern capitalists. Nevertheless, Yulee had everything to lose--his railroad had hardly begun to operate and it badly needed revenue from northern passengers and freight.

Former Congressman S.S. Cox would write after the war that neither Yulee nor Mallory were regarded as favorable to secession, "however they seemed." The reluctant Florida senators, nevertheless were loyal Floridians. Yulee wrote to the Legislature that if Florida seceded he would "promptly and joyously" return to the state.

Yulee's colleague, Stephen Mallory, had looked for compromise and didn't really cooperate with secessionists until Florida quit the union, following South Carolina and Mississippi. And so when the southerners caucused on Jan. 5, he and Yulee attended. The two Floridians notified Gov. Perry on Jan. 15 that they had ceased to participate in Senatorial activities, finally quitting the Senate on Jan. 21.

Yulee made a speech replete with lawyerish phrases: the state of Florida had been born out of land acquired from Spain under terms that said the inhabitants were to be admitted to the union on equal footing with other U.S. citizens; the act of 1845 admitting her to the union granted this equality. Thus in seceding, Florida was exercising her equal rights, he claimed.

Mallory, speaking emotionally, said: "We seek not war upon or to conquer you and we know that you cannot conquer us."

Before Yulee was to leave Washington, there would be unavailing attempts to call peace conferences. Governor Henry Wise of Virginia called delegates to a Washington peace conference. Yulee's elderly father-in-law, Charles Wickliffe, was chairman of the conference rules committee. Former President John Tyler was named president of the meeting. Some of Yulee's friends, attorney Reverdy Johnson of Maryland, and David S. Reid of North Carolina, also participated.

In New York, August Belmont--who had helped finance Yulee's railroad--also held a peace conference to enlist northern support. Many northerners had investments they were anxious to protect and New York Mayor Fernando Wood wanted to maintain trade ties. But both peace conferences were failures.

After quitting the Senate, Yulee journeyed southward, meeting with southern officials as he headed toward Florida. When he reached Fernandina in February, he sent Jefferson Davis a congratulatory letter. Davis had already been chosen Confederate president at Montgomery, Alabama.

"...Your election has quieted concern and raised the popular heart in hopefulness. I doubt if Washington in his day had more hold upon public confidence," Yulee wrote.

David Levy Yulee was once again back in Florida to pursue his obsession -- the railroad. More specifically, he sought to prevent its destruction in the ensuing war.

11

Moses Elias Levy had grown old. Though he had been unable to build a new Jerusalem in Florida or make good on his dream of establishing a boarding school for Jewish children, he had fought always to advance the status of Jews in America. Neither marauding Indians, nor legal battles, nor financial setbacks had kept him from becoming a major landowner and developer of pioneer Florida.

His worst problem was his family life: he was virtually estranged from his daughters, still living in the Caribbean, and, though he had reconciled with his youngest son, Sen. David Levy Yulee, the break with his older son, Elias, had never truly healed. True, he had risen to defend David against "inconceivable lies" when the son had been accused of being an "alien," but he bemoaned the fact that the younger son would not carry on the Jewish traditions.

Moses Levy had lived a monastic life. He lived apart from his wife for three years before his divorce. He never remarried and the only semblance of family life he recaptured was with his son, David and his wife, Nancy. From 1838 to 1841 he had lived alone in New York City before returning to St. Augustine.

As much as Moses Levy may have personally objected, David Levy Yulee's drift from orthodoxy was not an isolated phenomenon. Rabbi Malcolm Stern estimates that 15% of the Jews in the U.S. married Christians prior to 1840. Among Jews who attained public prominence, like banker August Belmont as well as Sen. Judah P. Benjamin, intermarriage was common.

In pre-Civil War America it was frequently true--as was said of Louisiana-- "there are Jews but no Judaism." There certainly was no central Jewish organization to guide Jews and no chief Rabbi, so that individual Jews followed their consciences in all matters, religious or political. Thanks to Rebecca Gratz, there was a Jewish Sunday school in Philadelphia by 1838. Isaac Leeser, also of Philadelphia, published the first national journal of Jewish news. But in the deep South, Jews were often isolated and on their own.

When David Levy Yulee went to the Senate in 1845, there were probably less than 50,000 Jews in America. By the time Judah P. Benjamin joined him there in 1853, there were about 58,000 to 60,000 Jews, but they still represented a small minority group in the young nation. From 1848 onward, immigration of Jews from Germany and western Europe increased markedly so that by the Civil War there were 150,000 in the states.

Florida was all but empty of Jews when Moses Levy arrived. There had been Jews in Pensacola and Mobile, Ala. as early as 1763, when West Florida was British. Joseph de Palacios and his partners, Samuel Israel and Alexander Solomons, were documented arrivals in Florida late in 1763. In the 1780's, a Jewish trader name Abraham Mordecai, who is said to be one of the pioneers who settled Mobile, Ala., married a Creek Indian woman and lived in west Florida. There may have been Jews in both Floridas even earlier. Who knows how many Marranos (forced converts who remained secret Jews) were among the 16th century Spanish arrivals-- men who whispered "yo soy un judio" to themselves at night.

Isaac and Manuel Monsanto were Jews who went to Pensacola after being expelled from Louisiana because of their religion but returned to New Orleans in 1758.

The West Florida House of Assembly passed a law on Dec. 22, 1766 to encourage foreign settlement, which provided for naturalization after three months. The law was meant to encourage settlement by French Catholics but it applied to Jews as well. Synagogues didn't exist in Florida until after the Civil War, however.

Moses Elias Levy was among the first Jews to take citizenship in the newly American territory of Florida and was uncritically welcomed to St. Augustine. Levy's attorney, George Fairbanks, stated that "His probity, large intelligence, and benevolence were recognized by all. I held him in the highest regard and veneration. He was very fond of children who were attracted to him. He was just and generous in his business transactions."

The elder Levy, in his later years, had intended to make Fairbanks his executor, but never got around to drawing a new will. Thus, when he died from a heart attack on Sept. 7, 1854, while visiting at Hot Springs, Virginia, he left an estate that did not reflect his new-found love for David Levy Yulee and his family. Moses Levy had been an American for better than three decades when he died at the age of 73.

Although his lands had been tied up in litigation for a decade, Moses Levy emerged from this situation richer in land than in dollars. Nevertheless, many of his years in St. Augustine were spent in local philanthropy. He campaigned for local free schools, for instance, although he was a desultory voter.

The will Moses Levy left behind provided only $100 to each of his four children. It directed that the remainder of his estate be sold, with the profits to be divided equally between his two daughters and his sister, Rachel (Mrs. Joseph Benlisa.) His sons, Elias and David, were both cut out of this distribution. The will named as executors, A.P. Henriques, a son-in-law living in St. Thomas, and two men from St. Augustine, Dr. Andrew Anderson and B.B. Putnam.

Neither Putnam nor Dr. Anderson ever acted as executors. After probate was transferred from Virginia to St. Augustine, David Levy Yulee made application to take charge. He was named administrator along with John F. Fontaine and John E. Peek.

On March 11, 1857, David and Elias Yulee brought suit to break the will. The court case was transferred to Madison, Fla. Oddly, all the court records disappeared after they were transferred from St. Augustine to Madison, but it appears that Elias ultimately received more than $12,000 in cash and bonds and the sisters received $15,000. David granted all of his interest in the estate to Elias "in consideration of brotherly affection."

He was also to write a long narrative explanation of the family history as administrator in which he told how, having supported himself during his father's life, he also did not take "any part of the estate he left," despite having "performed a considerable amount of business service for him before our separation and afterward, without remuneration."

When David Levy Yulee assumed administration of the estate, he was the only child living in Florida. He feared his brother would be excluded from any inheritance from his father, "for there had been no revival of their natural relations. Knowing my father's peculiar religious views and theory of life, which had unhappily broken up the family and scattered and alienated its members, I considered that it would not be right to exclude my brother from his just and proper share," he wrote.

Elias Levy had lived in Georgia, volunteered for the Confederate army (Washington Rifles) and eventually moved to the Washington territory. A grandson, Samuel Yulee Way, later became a mayor of Orlando.

At death, Moses Elias Levy owned land in Marion, Alachua, Volusia, Orange, Duval and Sumter Counties, totaling 77,251 acres. Moses Levy did make an effort prior to his death to share some of his money holdings with David but there is no confirmation this was consummated. Levy wrote to David Naar, a commercial agent in New York, directing him to sell some of his stocks and give the proceeds to David.

Moses Elias Levy's will did not actually go to probate until 1915, more than 60 years after his death, the distribution of the estate having been worked out between the surviving children.

Moses Levy's chosen surname remains on the Florida map. Levy County on the west coast of Florida is one of the more rural of the state's 67 counties. It is, however, named after David, who bore the name of Levy for 35 years before he changed his name. Cedar Key is still its best-known community, though it is not the county seat. There is also a Levy Lake near Micanopy, in Alachua County, where Moses Levy established his first plantation. There once was a town called Levyville, no longer on the state map. The city of Sanford, Fla. is situated on land which was once known as the M.E. Levy grant.

The Yulee surname is commemorated by the small town of Yulee, near the Georgia border in east Florida. There is a Yulee Drive in Old Homosassa and the remains of Yulee's sugar mill are preserved here in a state park. Historical marketer at Fernandina and Cedar Key also commemorate the railroad. Yulee's rail station at Fernandina still stands as well. It houses the Chamber of Commerce. Yulee's real estate development firm, the Town Improvement Co. created the town of Archer, near Gainesville. It is named after his colleague on the Internal Improvement Fund Board, James T. Archer.

Yet neither Moses Levy nor David Levy Yulee occupy any special niche in the memory of most Floridians. Some say that early historians were reluctant to give David as much credit as he deserved for bringing Florida into statehood and for building the first cross-state railroad simply because of his Jewish roots. Yet many other pioneer Floridians are not remembered either. The once empty Florida now has 1,000 new residents arriving each day. Perhaps because of this epidemic rate of settlement, Floridians are becoming much more aware of their history and environment and interested in preserving a record of the past.

If that is the case, then Moses Levy, the "Hebrew visionary," as Achille Murat called him, deserves recognition as a man who saw Florida's residential and agricultural potential before it was ceded to the U.S. by Spain--a man who foresaw east Florida as a homeland of the Jews 127 years before there was an Israel.

More certainly, David Levy Yulee's place in the Florida and national pantheons is well earned. If any one man in the Florida territory was able to bring order out of chaos, it was David, who led the settlers into statehood in 1845. Like his father, he knew defeat and frustration many times, yet persisted. In 1860, his cross-Florida railroad linked two coasts of the peninsula, doing in miniature what the transcontinental railroad did for the nation in 1869.

12

Modern readers may wonder why Moses Elias Levy, a religious Jew, and his son, Sen. David Levy Yulee, accepted slavery and worked slaves at a time when two-thirds of white Floridians owned none. Most poor whites who had land worked small plots aided only by family members. Plantation owners like Moses Elias Levy and his son simply assumed it to be right and normal that slaves were required to work their large holdings.

If Moses Levy thought slavery wrong, he and his son shared common rationalizations about the necessity of slaves--they were allegedly immune to malaria and yellow fever; they could tolerate the heat and humidity and toil under conditions other workers rejected. In their minds, slavery was an institution that had been accepted by Aristotle and the founding fathers.

In truth, the fact that both men came from a Caribbean culture reinforced a plantation mentality based on sugar. Sugar was a recognized pathway to wealth but it was a demanding crop which could be worked only by the hardiest of men. Ergo, slaves over whites or even native Indians. Sugar cane came to the Caribbean with

Columbus on his second voyage and this crop--as much as cotton--perpetuated slavery after coming to America.

David Levy Yulee had as many as 100 slaves working at his Homosassa sugar plantation. His colleague in the Senate, Judah P. Benjamin, had 140 slaves at his sugar plantation near New Orleans. A former Floridian, Raphael J. Moses, of St. Joseph and Apalachicola, was a Jew who had slaves at his Esquiline plantation in Columbus, Ga.

Most Jews in the South, however, lived in towns and were merchants, not plantation owners. Therefore very few owned slaves.

Reputed to be a kind master, David Levy Yulee once referred to slaves as "three millions of beings placed by Providence under our guardianship." He clearly enjoyed the social status that slave ownership conferred on plantation owners but tended to couch his defense of the institution in legalisms.

Eli Evans has noted in "The Provincials" that southern Jews shared the views of their Christian neighbors in acceptance of slavery. The only documented southern Jew who was an abolitionist was Marx E. Lazarus of North Carolina--and even he enlisted in the Confederate army.

Some European Jews, who had fought for freedom as overseas revolutionaries in Austria and Hungary, vigorously opposed slavery after they immigrated to America. August Bondi fought with John Brown in Kansas and used his Missouri home as a station in the Underground Railway. A supporter of John C. Fremont name Michael Heilprin was an outspoken critic of the "peculiar institution." Heilprin had fought with Kossuth in Hungary. Bondi was a freedom fighter as a student in Austria.

Even rabbis were divided. David Einhorn, an anti-slavery rabbi in Baltimore, was nearly killed by a mob for speaking his views. Yet Morris J. Raphall, of New York, who was honored on Feb. 1, 1860 as the first rabbi in history to offer a prayer at an opening session of Congress, also delivered a sermon in 1861 that claimed the Bible provided justification for slavery.

Raphall's invocation in Congress triggered a wave of invective directed at Sens. Yulee and Benjamin, highly visible as the only senators of Jewish descent. Their mutual inattention to Judaism availed them nothing. They were the number one targets in the gallery of bigotry.

First, however, came barbed wit from an anonymous New York Times reporter, who wrote: "The Christian religion having failed to produce an organization, resort is now had to a learned rabbi, who appears in full canonicals, and delivers a very excellent prayer. Ben Perley Poore, who sits beside me, suggests that this is the result of the irrepressible conflict...others give the affair a political signification and suspect that Mr. (Jonas) Levy, of this city, is laying pipes for a ticket to consist of Senators Benjamin and Yulee as the president and vice president of Southern Jerusalem..."

But soon satirical jibes were followed by truly nasty insults: At the outbreak of secession, the abolitionist Boston Transcript referred to Benjamin as a Jewish traitor and added "Mr. Yulee of Florida, whose name has been changed from the more appropriate one of Levy, has always been one of the hottest leaders of the ultra fire-eaters..."

One of the worst comments was made on Feb. 28, 1861 (after Florida seceded) by Sen. Andrew Johnson of Tennessee, who was yet to be inaugurated vice president. He said to Charles Francis Adams: "There's that Yulee, miserable little cuss! I remember him in the House--that contemptible little Jew--standing there and begging us--yes! begging us to let Florida in as a state. Well! We let her in and took care of her, and fought her Indians, and now that despicable little beggar stands up in the Senate and talks about her rights." Johnson had even more to say about Benjamin, adding: "There's another Jew--that miserable Benjamin! He looks on a country and a government as he would a suit of old clothes. He sold out the old one; and he would sell out the new if he could, in so doing, make two or three millions."

The Tennessean, who was once a poor tailor and made his own suits when he first came to Congress, lumped Yulee in with the loudest of the secessionists despite his subsequent moderation.

Senator Edward Bates called Yulee a "treacherous Jew" in 1862 and Gideon Welles, who was Lincoln's Secretary of the Navy, accused Yulee of having narrow and mercenary talents used mostly "in obtaining local favors from the government for his state and himself."

Rabbi Raphall gave his slavery defense sermon when President Buchanan called for a national day of prayer to forestall secession. His sermon, "The Bible

View of Slavery," claimed the 10 commandments authorized slavery. According to Rabbi Raphall, slaves were the sons of Ham who bore a curse. "How dare you denounce slavery as a sin?," he said, "When you remember that Abraham, Isaac, Jacob, Job, the men with whom the Almighty conversed...that all these men were slave holders. Does it not strike you that you are guilty of something very little short of blasphemy?"

Raphall was denounced by many Jews as a "knave and a fool," and Baltimore's Rabbi Einhorn asked if God had shown any respect for "historic right" when he freed the Hebrews from slavery in Egypt.

Still, Rabbi Isaac Mayer Wise of Cincinnati was to attack abolitionists as "fanatics, demagogues and demons of hatred and destruction..." Abolitionist newspapers and members of Congress were particularly vicious in their attacks on Jews and Wise considered them to be dangerous extremists. "Too often," he note, "those who faint away on hearing of a Negro thousands of miles distant having been abused, are always ready to wrong their next neighbor..."

"Do you know who made Jefferson Davis and the Rebellion?," he was to ask, "The priests (clergy) did, and their whiners and howlers in the press."

Though he opposed ministers participating in the "vulgar business of politics," Rabbi Wise was, himself, a "peace Democrat." Because Judah P. Benjamin went on to be "the brains of the Confederacy," holding three cabinet posts, he ultimately became more of a lightning rod for anti-Semitic attack than Yulee, who did not serve in the Confederate government.

Benjamin came to the Senate eight years after Yulee arrived in 1845. His most recent biographer, Eli Evans, considers him to be the first Jewish senator because he never renounced his faith, though Rabbi Bertram W. Korn, in his sketch on Benjamin's Jewishness, concludes that he was at best "indifferent" to his religion. Yulee never made a formal conversion to Christianity, either. Benjamin kept strong ties to this family, who remained Jewish, but he was totally non-observant. Yulee shrank from Judaism because of the zealous religious views of his father.

There are many parallels in the respective backgrounds of the two senators. They were born a year apart on adjoining islands in what are now the Virgins. Both came from Sephardic antecedents. Both grew to maturity as loners removed from Jewish influences. They became friends while serving in the Senate and their lives followed similar tracks in neighboring southern states.

David Levy Yulee was born on St. Thomas June 2, 1810, while Judah P. Benjamin was born on St. Croix on Aug. 11, 1811. Their fathers knew one another--Benjamin's father's name (Philip) appears on legal papers connected with Moses Elias Levy's divorce. Judah P. Benjamin's uncle, Emanuel, was a business partner of Moses Levy. Both boys left their island homes as children and grew up in America. Judah P. Benjamin grew up in towns in North and South Carolina, principally Charleston. David Levy Yulee spent his formative years in Norfolk, Va. and Micanopy, Fla.

Benjamin had two years at Yale before leaving under peculiar circumstances, though Benjamin himself blamed his father's financial reverses for ending his collegiate years. He was 16 when he went to New Orleans, subsequently deciding to become a lawyer on his own resources. David Levy Yulee was cut off from higher education by his father at age 17 and, like Benjamin, studied law on his own. Both men made their mark in booming states of the deep South. Both were sugar planters, both railroad planners, both married Christian women and both endured anti-Semitic slurs despite lives removed from Jewish observance.

As lawyer and statesman, however, Benjamin's national fame eclipsed that of Yulee. Politically they had come to power in opposite camps. Yulee was a populist who fought Florida's elite Whigs and their banks, while Benjamin was from the outset a southern Whig in cosmopolitan New Orleans. They came together in defense of slavery as senators. Thought Yulee had been a fire-eating disciple of John C. Calhoun in his first term both he and Benjamin were among the moderates in the final hotheaded days before secession. Yulee underwent a gradual transformation from radical Democrat to landed gentry man. Benjamin, it appears, aspired to this status from the start.

Yulee, however, enjoyed a good family life and raised four children. His wife, Nancy, was a prominent Washington, D.C. and Florida socialite. Benjamin had only one child by his wife, Natalie, who with her daughter, Ninette, lived in Paris apart from her husband for most of their marriage.

The friendship of Yulee and Benjamin had one of its strongest tests when the Louisiana senator initially came to Washington, renting the famed house on Lafayette Square where Stephen Decatur once lived and furnishing it lavishly. He hoped to settle Natalie amid plush surroundings and introduce her to the society life which she craved. But Washington's society snubbed her--and passed the rumor that she was romantically involved with a French officer.

Crushed, Benjamin considered quitting Washington, until Yulee talked him out of it--according to Robert Douthat Meade, a biographer of Benjamin. Then he put up all the furnishings of the Decatur house for auction. Mrs. Yulee bought most of them and they were shipped to "Marguerita," the Yulee mansion home on Tiger Tail Island in Homosassa. Yulee's daughter, Florida (Mrs. Wallace Neff), confirmed the story of Mrs. Benjamin's Washington misadventures many years later in an interview.

Natalie Benjamin returned to Paris and never came back to the United States, though Benjamin was to visit her annually for years--mostly to see Ninette, on whom he doted. Yet in Washington, he was a lonely workaholic with a penchant for gambling and gourmet dining. According to Meade, he had few intimates with the exception of Yulee, his Louisiana colleague John Slidell, and Sen. James A. Bayard of Delaware. Benjamin liked to drop in at the Yulee home on Saturdays. "Benjamin was very fond of Yulee," Meade wrote.

13

If David Levy Yulee's views on slavery comported with the prevailing attitudes in the South, he also shared the common opinion that the South was being hemmed in by the aggressive industrial North. He feared that states like Florida would lose their way of life. He believed Florida would be "Africanized" if slaves were freed. This, too, was the conventional southern wisdom of the day.

Two weeks after the election, Yulee sent a letter to the Florida legislature saying that if Florida seceded before the expiration of his term on March 4, 1861, "I shall promptly and joyously return home to support the banner of my state to which my allegiance is owing and in which my family altar is established."

Of course, he already knew that was exactly what Florida intended to do if Lincoln was elected. In 1856, Florida Democrats had declared that Congressional prohibition of slavery would amount to "intolerable oppression and justify a resort to measures of resistance." In 1860, they were even more radical, nominating planter John Milton to be governor. Milton was so fervent a secessionist that he shot himself in 1865, eight days before Robert E. Lee surrendered. Milton's predecessor, Madison S. Perry, had signed a bill calling for secession shortly after Lincoln's election. He convened a special state convention for early January, 1861, to vote on the question.

Prior to the convention, Maj. John Beard--who had been an unsuccessful Democratic candidate for Congress--invited Edmund Ruffin to Tallahassee "for the pleasure of seeing Florida withdraw from the union." Ruffin, a Virginia-born agricultural scientist, had given up his work on soil to become a full time agitator for secession. It was Ruffin who fired the first shot at Ft. Sumter in April, starting the bloody Civil War.

But three months earlier, having arrived in Tallahassee at Beard's invitation, the hot-blooded Ruffin became angry when the Florida secession convention delayed action. It didn't meet until Jan. 5--having delayed because President Buchanan called a national day of "fasting and humiliation" the previous day, hoping to defer the inevitable.

Though Florida voted to secede on Jan. 7, 1861--the third southern state to do so--Ruffin was so enraged at the delay in Florida's action that he refused to attend a special church service which had been called to bless the departure. (He, too, shot himself at the end of the Civil War.)

Even the Episcopal Bishop of Florida, South Carolina-born Francis H. Rutledge, was caught up in secession hysteria. He sent to the convention a personal promise to pay $500 to the state to help defray the expenses of secession. Rutledge shared the passions of another Episcopal bishop, Leonidas Polk, who became a

Confederate general and was killed in the war.

It was on Jan. 5 that Sen. Yulee wrote his fateful letter to Gen. Joseph Finnegan (his railroad associate and a member of the state convention), urging immediate occupation of the U.S. forts in Florida. This letter was used after the collapse of the Confederacy as alleged proof of Yulee's "treason" by Judge Advocate General Joseph Holt. Yulee's accusers ignored the fact that he also wrote Gov. Perry on Jan.20 asking that "there be no bloodshed" in counseling against an attack against union-held Ft. Pickens.

Holt had married into the slave-holding Wickliffe family and believed, with Yulee, that slavery was sanctioned by the Constitution. Holt was a Kentuckian who had also lived in Mississippi. Nevertheless, he was a pro-union absolutist who believed that secessionists were traitors. Just before the Finnegan letter, Holt had refused a request by Yulee and Sen. Mallory to furnish them an inventory of munitions and equipment held in the Florida forts and arsenals.

Yulee and Holt also exchanged angry letters over the conduct of a Florida militiaman, Col. William C. Chase, who was interrupting mail service between Washington, D.C. and Ft. Pickens, despite a promise from Yulee that mail would not be interfered with. To Holt, Chase's actions were "treasonable and despicable" and he blamed Yulee, breaking off further communications with him.

This fight between brothers-in-law may explain as well as anything Yulee's bellicose letter to Finnegan. Yet on Jan. 9, Yulee also introduced a bill in the Senate to "Facilitate the peaceful adjustment of controversies between the states of the union."

As high as secession fever ran in Florida, it was not totally unanimous. The final ordinance of secession passed the convention by a 62-7 vote on January 10. Among the most outspoken opponents was former Territorial Gov. Richard Keith Call. In 1860, Call had written a public letter, invoking the spirit of Andrew Jackson and warning "if you go further you will commit treason against your country and trample on the grave of Andrew Jackson." After secession had been voted, some jubilant delegates came by Call's home to exult, "Well, Governor, we have done it!"

Call responded, "And what have you done? You have opened the gates of hell, from which shall flow the curses of the damned which shall send you to perdition!"

Despite the provocative letter to Gen. Finnegan, Yulee had also urged Jefferson Davis to reconsider his refusal to serve on the Committee of 13, which considered several peace plans. Among them was Kentucky Senator John J. Crittenden's plan which called for a Yulee-like amendment to the Constitution to preserve slavery. In these hectic days, those who sought compromise tried everything--peace conferences, last minute appeals to southern and border states which hadn't called secession conventions, even a government-sponsored colonization plan for free Negroes.

(Colonization was an idea that went back to James Madison and early 19th century Virginia, where a colonization society was formed which tried to resettle 200 slaves. It was an idea to which Abraham Lincoln also subscribed in the search for answers prior to the war.)

But these were the days of the hotspur. Moderation was impossible.

14

By 1860 Florida's political climate reached the point where, as Rembert W. Patrick described it, "unity and conformity in defense of the institution of slavery were demanded...(and) freedom of speech and press where the institution was questioned could not be tolerated." Yulee had grown sick of elective politics by this time.

He had been nursing the idea of retiring at the end of his term. Secession thus allowed him to leave Washington one month earlier than he might have. His second term would have expired on March 4, 1861. In a letter of May 10, 1860 to Col. J.B. Brown of Key West, he had, in fact, announced his intention to retire, saying he had spent 16 of the last 20 years in public office.

He added, "I do not believe my health will longer endure the climate of this latitude, and after so much absence from Florida, I am naturally solicitous to enjoy at last the pleasures of home life." This was somewhat disingenuous, since it was to Washington that he returned near the end of his life.

Nevertheless, when the letter was printed in the St. Augustine Examiner, the editor opined that Yulee's retirement would be "a disappointment in ordinary times but in the present volcanic one, it is tragic." The paper said Yulee had been "Faithful, devoted to truth, to the Constitution and to his constituents through 20 stormy years and no man's public career has been more dignified, successful and satisfactory than his...we think it is safe to say that to no one man in the state are the people of Florida (more) indebted for their prosperity than to Hon. David L. Yulee..."

On his final day in the Senate, Yulee was the first southern Senator to announce his withdrawal. He was followed by Mallory, Sens. Clement Clay and Benjamin Fitzpatrick of Alabama, and Jefferson Davis of Mississippi. Yulee returned to Florida in February.

The outbreak of was soon galvanized Yulee into action to protect his railroad. On July 20, 1861, one day after the first battle of Manassas, he wrote to his friend, Gov. Francis W. Pickens of South Carolina, requesting an artillery battery to supplement the Florida troops being raised by Gen. Finnegan in east Florida. First Manassas was a smashing southern victory and had shattered union hopes that the war would end with one decisive battle. Conversely, it gave the rebs inordinate hope of victory over the North. But Yulee also knew that Fernandina and Cedar Key would become early targets for a union Navy that overwhelmingly outclassed what few ships the South had.

So, in October, he went to the Confederate capital at Richmond to negotiate with Judah P. Benjamin on the defense of Fernandina. Benjamin had just become Secretary of War, after serving as attorney general, and found himself woefully short of resources. Yet the potential loss of the Atlantic rail terminus at Fernandina was disturbing to him. The port got some fortification but not what Yulee had hoped for.

On Jan. 15, 1862, federal forces raided Cedar Key on the Gulf of Mexico. A lone gunboat, the U.S. Hatteras, entered the harbor and discovered it to be virtually undefended. The ship sent in a shore party which spiked three cannons and burned the railroad depot, seven freight cars and a turpentine warehouse. Five schooners and three sloops loaded with cotton and turpentine were also torched. Telegraph wires were pulled down and Cedar Key was left in a shambles.

Hearing of the raid, Yulee left Fernandina by train the following day to arrange for evacuation of women and children. Before he left Fernandina, he wired Benjamin to provide 10-inch guns for protection of the Atlantic terminus.

Mrs. Yulee and the children were sent from Fernandina to "Marguerita," the family plantation at Homosassa. Here Yulee had begun his sugar plantation in 1851 and built a sugar mill. He had also collected and grown rare flowers, plants and fruits at Homosassa. The mansion house was on an island at the mouth of the Homosassa River, once the headquarters of a Seminole chief. Mrs. Yulee and the children often swam or relaxed under the shade of the giant "Yulee Oak" which stood near the shore.

Yulee, however, remained in Fernandina and continued to bombard Confederate authorities with requests for troops and guns. Neither his friend

Benjamin nor his former colleague Mallory could provide much help.

On March 3, 1862, a squadron of naval gunboats made their way southward from Port Royal, S.C. into the harbor at Fernandina, having come in the back way to avoid the fortifications. As the vessels approached, a train was assembled and soon packed with inhabitants and their household goods. Yulee boarded the last car. Just as the train started across the trestle from Amelia Island, the Ottawa--the lead gunboat--opened fire. A solid shot struck the car Yulee was in, killing a man next to him and maiming another.

Yulee was unhurt and able to scramble out of the train. The damaged car was uncoupled and the train kept going. The trestle was burned after the train crossed. It was Yulee's closest personal encounter with warfare.

He rejoined his family at Homosassa and relocated the Florida Railroad offices from Fernandina to Gainesville a few days later. Five days after the evacuation of Fernandina, and nearly three months after the raid on Cedar Key, Yulee and citizens of central Florida petitioned Richmond to station troops of sufficient strength to protect east Florida. They also asked that the few troops then in the area be allowed to remain and that Gen. T.H. Trapier, commander of east Florida troops, be removed for "apparent incapacity or want of industry."

Surprisingly, Yulee agreed to a resolution which would allow destruction of such portions of the railroad as might be deemed necessary to prevent the advance of the enemy. Yet, when Gov. Milton sent down orders two days later to remove the rails and transport them for use at a Lake City junction with the

Tallahassee line, Yulee objected.

Yulee had fought hard in the past to keep his railroad apart from Georgia competition and the war hadn't changed his position. On March 24, Milton declared he would arrest anybody who tried to prevent the rail removal, adding: "if necessary, inform me and I will declare martial law in east Florida forthwith."

This enraged Yulee and on April 12, he obtained a court injunction which stopped the track removal--at least for the next two years. However, in 1864 the Confederacy ignored Yulee and the courts and began to pull up the tracks, anyway. At this stage of the war, the Confederacy was nearing desperation. Resources had dwindled and supply lines shrunk.

It was the spring of 1864 when the Confederate War Department decided to complete a rail connection between the Pensacola & Georgia Railroad and the Atlantic & Gulf Railroad, from Live Oak, Fla. to DuPont, Ga. Lacking the rails to accomplish this, it was decided to "impress" Yulee's rails. When an engineering officer named Lt. Jason M. Fairbanks started to carry out the order, Yulee filed suit against Fairbanks, Secretary of War James Seddon and others, including Confederate Navy Secretary Stephen Mallory, his former Senate colleague.

The court awarded the injunction but Fairbanks ignored the writ on orders from his commander, impounding a locomotive and cars to haul away the rails. An attempt was made to bring Fairbanks into court on contempt charges, but in the end Yulee's efforts to use the civilian courts came to nothing. Federal troops actually stopped the Confederates from tearing up more rails.

Yulee still clung to his domain. Since 1862, he had commuted by horse and buggy from Homosassa to Gainesville, about 80 miles, to keep segments of the railroad operating. Once, in August, 1864, federal troops were sent to try and capture Yulee, but he escaped when one of his Kentucky bay horses got sick and he substituted a brace of mules for motive power. He rode undetected right past the intended ambush.

In 1863, Yulee had another contretemps with Confederate authority. The city of Savannah, Ga. had contracted with him to provide 64 hogsheads of sugar, nearly 50,000 pounds, for $1.10 per pound for first quality and $1 a pound for second. A Confederate commissary officer named Antonio A. Canova seized the sugar at the Waldo rail station while it was en route to Savannah.

In July, Canova offered to pay Yulee 45 cents a pound for the seized sugar, but Yulee refused to accept this low price. Besides, he said, he had offered the sugar to the Confederate government before selling it to Savannah and it was declined. He also said he had 16,000 more pounds in storage at Gainesville and if the government needed sugar it could purchase this sugar without resorting to impressment.

Canova's response was to order the Waldo station agent to hold Yulee's sugar under armed guard. Agents for the city of Savannah filed suit for damages but their case was dismissed. An appraisal of the seized sugar was ordered, which fixed a price of $1.08 a pound or $54,204.19 for the lot. This time Canova objected to the price and a special commission was selected to adjust the prices. It fixed a price of 75 cents a pound, to which Yulee now objected. He filed suit at Savannah in

October. The judge upheld the $1.08 price but said it should have been set when the sugar was seized in April. Claiming the judge erred in granting final judgment, Yulee appealed to the Georgia Supreme Court which, in 1864, sent the case back to the lower court. There is no record of final disposition and it is presumed Yulee never did collect a dime.

For Yulee, these were bitter times. Between the union army and his friends in the Confederate government, he was rapidly losing his shirt. In May of 1864, he was to lose even more--his mansion and all of its fine possessions. The paintings and silver acquired from Judah P. Benjamin's house in Washington, as well as an excellent library, were destroyed when the house was torched by union raiders. For some time Yulee had been paying infantry to guard the house but they had been withdrawn. Household slaves saved a few objects, but not much.

This loss occurred while the Yulee family was visiting friends, Mr. and Mrs. James Taylor, in Ocala. A messenger came to them from Homosassa on May 30, 1864. He reported that Yankee soldiers had destroyed the house and taken everything of value that remained. House servants had been warned by the barking of "Secesh," the family dog, and escaped. They hid in the woods and from there saw a column of black smoke, indicating that "Marguerita" was no longer standing.

The sugar plantation and mill hadn't been destroyed, so Yulee arranged to hire an overseer while he moved his family to Gainesville. Their friend, Mrs. Marie Taylor, with whom they had been staying at Ocala, said Mrs. Yulee bore the loss of her home "with much Christian fortitude." The Yulee family moved in with Mrs. Taylor's daughter-except for Wickliffe, who remained at the Taylor home recovering from malaria. Three weeks later Sen. Yulee moved the family to a new home called "Cottonwood," which he purchased along with 160 acres of land, at Archer near Gainesville.

Yulee, despite his losses, kept busy with business affairs. Aware that the South was critically short of iron, he organized the Yulee Manufacturing Co. in 1863 to mine low grad iron ore found near the surface of the ground in Levy County, but the project failed. However, he managed to make money by trading with Cuba to circumvent the union blockade throttling Florida. He made nearly $4,000 in two months on an investment of $1,433. This trading was sanctioned by the Confederacy, for it enabled them to get medicines and other critically short supplies.

Nevertheless, friends were also falling in the war, including George W. Call, who had been secretary of the railroad. Call was killed at the Battle of Seven Pines in Virginia.

Florida had been a breadbasket for the Confederacy, providing beef as well as salt and sugar. It was never a major battle area. But with the end of the war nearing, the state experienced a few skirmishes and one big battle, the fight at Olustee (Ocean Pond) which ended in a union defeat. At the very end, however, everything was in a shambles. Robert E. Lee surrendered on April 9, 1865. Yulee's friend, Gen. Joseph Johnston, surrendered his forces in North Carolina on April 26. Union troops were to occupy Florida well into 1866, however.

Governor Milton died by his own hand on April 1, 1865, so Acting Gov.

Abraham K. Allison took a bold step. He decided to appoint five special commissioners who were to proceed to Washington, obtain an interview with the President and seek Florida's readmission to the union.

Allison named David Levy Yulee to be one of the commissioners. Allison requested union Gen. J. H. Wilson to provide them with passports and went ahead with setting a special session of the Florida legislature to elect a governor on June 7. Commanding General E.M McCook had other ideas. He told Wilson, "You will not recognize the so-called governor or any of his officers purporting to act under his orders..." All of Florida was placed under martial law.

Northerners meanwhile whispered that Yulee might help them with Reconstruction because of his several disputes with the Confederacy.

Concurrently, Jefferson Davis and his cabinet had evacuated Richmond and were following a ragged course southward, hoping to escape. The assassination of Lincoln within days of Appomattox had put their lives in jeopardy. After fleeing Richmond, Davis had sent some trunks full of personal mementos and Confederate papers to Yulee for safekeeping.

This shipment reached "Cottonwood" on the evening of May 22, 1865, 12 days after Davis had been captured in Georgia and taken in chains to prison. Originally it was hoped that the Davis papers would be sent on either to Texas or to some port in Florida, where they could be sent to safety in Nassau.

Mrs. Yulee told the Confederate party which had brought the trunks about Davis' capture. The party broke up, leaving the papers behind. After a nocturnal attempt to bury the trunks in the yard at "Cottonwood," they were sent, at Yulee's direction, to M.A. Williams, the station agent at Waldo, where they ultimately passed into federal hands.

A detachment of black union troops was sent to "Cottonwood" about the same time to retrieve Davis' property, only to be told the trunks had already gone to Waldo. Mrs. Yulee gave the officer in charge a French musket which she said belonged to Davis and which had been part of the shipment. Despite his past legal tiffs with the Confederacy, Yulee felt it was only proper for him to safeguard Davis' property. To do otherwise would have seemed petty, he said.

Yulee also intended to carry out Allison's instructions. But before he could proceed, he was arrested on May 25, 1865 and taken to military headquarters at Jacksonville. Yulee thought he would be taken from Jacksonville to Washington and tried. Knowing how sentiment in the capital was running, he arranged for his wife and children to go to her family home in Kentucky. She chose instead to go to relatives in Maryland to be nearer Washington.

However, on June 10, Yulee and Allison were sent to prison cells at Ft. Pulaski, Ga. Secretary of War Edwin M. Stanton reported to President Andrew Johnson that Yulee was imprisoned and charged with "treason while holding a seat in the U.S. Senate; with plotting to capture the forts and arsenals of the United States, and with inciting war and rebellion against the government."

Also reporting to Stanton was Judge Advocate General Joseph Holt, who counseled him to disregard requests for amnesty for his brother-in-law. In Holt's words, Yulee and Sen. Mallory had committed "overt acts of treason." He called for their trial, saying, "the atrocity of the machinations of these men is strikingly aggravated by their skulking treachery..."

Judge Holt, like Stanton, believed strongly in conspiracy theories. As head of the Military Bureau of Justice, he was the hanging judge who presided over the swift trial and execution of John Wilkes Booth's companions--one of whom was a Florida boy named Lewis Powell (also known as Lewis Payne, who had attacked but not killed Secretary of State William H. Seward the same night Booth shot Lincoln). This genuine plot had convinced Holt that treason was rampant in Dixie. He harshly suppressed evidence that might have saved the life of Mary Surratt, an alleged Booth co-conspirator.

Months of hard jail time lay ahead for Yulee--and for Mallory, who was imprisoned in New York's Ft. Lafayette. Every member of the Confederate cabinet went to jail, except for Judah P. Benjamin--who made an incredible escape from Florida to England--and John C. Breckenridge, Secretary of War, who also sailed from Florida to a refuge in Havana.

Just before Jefferson Davis was captured in Georgia, Benjamin left the cabinet group and rode to Florida disguised as a Frenchman. He hid in an attic in Tampa and then at Robert Gamble's mansion near Bradenton, repeatedly escaping capture.

From Sarasota Bay he embarked on a series of voyages that brought him near death three times from storms and sinkings. Ultimately he got to the Bahamas, then to Havana. After boarding a steamboat which caught fire and had to put in at St. Thomas for repairs, he ultimately sailed to England, never to return to the U.S.

Yulee's imprisonment was out of all proportion to his pre-secession Senate role or his wartime civilian status. He had not participated in the Confederate government. However unwise his letter to Gen. Finnegan had been, it was scarcely sufficient grounds for a charge of treason. But these were not times for clear thought. Vengeance was on the land.

15

Former Sen. David Levy Yulee was imprisoned at Ft. Pulaski for nine months, from June 19, 1865 to March 25, 1866. The island prison at the mouth of the Savannah River also held several former Confederate officials: James A. Seddon, one of the six secretaries of war; Treasurer G.A. Trenholm and Robert M.T. Hunter, a former Secretary of State. When he was finally released in 1866, Yulee was forbidden to leave Florida and had to report on a monthly basis to Judge Advocate General Joseph Holt. Later, his parole was modified so he could travel outside Florida.

Even though Yulee's jail term lasted only nine months compared to Jefferson Davis' two-year imprisonment he still had a hard time winning his release. It took a letter from former Confederate General Joseph Johnston to Ulysses S. Grant to actually get him out. Yulee's own applications for amnesty to President Andrew Johnson were ignored.

Yulee wrote the man who had once vilified him as a "miserable Jew" to plead that he had not been connected with any military or civil action of the

Confederacy. He also denied that he had left his Senate seat to help secession and rebellion.

The war, he wrote, had produced two incontrovertible facts, "that involuntary servitude is abolished forever, and that the union is national. I accept them in good faith and am prepared to aid their beneficial development." Gen. Israel Vogdes, a key union general in Florida, had written the President on July 11, 1865 to argue that Yulee belonged to the "peaceable secession party and was bitterly opposed to any resort to arms." Provisional Gov. William Martin pleaded for Yulee's release on grounds he was "president of a railroad company whose interests are suffering for the want of his supervision and care."

From prison, Yulee wrote his ex-colleague Stephen Mallory (who had been jailed at Ft. Lafayette in New York harbor) that "slave labor has been abolished and state sovereignty (has) become a phantasm." But Yulee's unyielding brother-in-law, Judge Advocate General Holt, remained adamant .

"These suggestions of clemency totally ignore the criminality of these men," cried Holt, who wanted "atonement" and punishment. Secretary of War Stanton, despite having represented both Yulee and his railroad, was equally untroubled by Yulee's plight.

There is irony in the fact that Yulee's successful bid for release had to be passed from a former Confederate general to Grant and thence to President Johnson. During the war, Grant had been so outraged by cotton speculations going on in Tennessee and Mississippi that he issued the Civil War's most blatantly anti-

Semitic document, the notorious Order #11, which ordered all Jews out of the Department of the Tennessee. Lincoln had it repealed after some Jews were thrown out of their homes and businesses in Mississippi, Tennessee and Kentucky.

Though there may have been individual Jews who were cotton speculators, this practice was hardly limited to one religion. Grant's own brother-in-law did some speculation. It was commonplace to accuse all speculators of being "Jews," however. Grant sputtered about them, as did his friend, Gen. William Tecumseh Sherman. Even Florida's Gov. John Milton wrote a letter to the Confederacy complaining about "vile Jews" and their trading practices. The Washington Chronicle called Jews "the scavengers of commerce."

Worse yet, the Associated Press transmitted a story which read: "The Jews of New Orleans and all the South ought to be exterminated. They run the blockade and are always to be found at the bottom of every new villainy."

Grant may have had no personal feelings against Yulee's Jewish roots. One of his close friends was Jesse Seligman, a prominent Jewish New York financier, whom he met before the war while a lieutenant stationed at Watertown, N.Y. After the war, he stated publicly that he held no bad feelings for any sect. In any case, Grant wrote to President Johnson on March 22, 1866, "respectfully recommending the release, on parole, of D.L. Yulee." Three days later Yulee was out of jail. He never went to trial despite the serious charges made against him. (Grant was honored by Yulee in 1880 when, as President, he came to Fernandina and attended a reception given by Mr. and Mrs. Yulee at the Egmont Hotel. Yulee co-owned the hotel, probably the first tourist hotel ever built in the state.)

Upon release from prison in 1866, Yulee faced incredible financial problems. He was 56 years old and all but wiped out. He owed a promissory note of $100,000 which had to be repaid. The railroad had a total debt of $5,483,000, including $1,432,000 in unpaid interest. It was estimated that restoration of the system to its former condition would cost more than the original construction.

The trestle to the mainland from Fernandina was destroyed and wharves, warehouses, depots and repair shops all along the line had been burned. Rails had been ripped up. Thirty-three of the first 40 miles of track were gone. Cross-ties had rotted and small bridges collapsed. The rolling stock had been depleted and only nine box cars and 12 flat cars remained. Three locomotives also remained.

While he was still in jail, Yulee began pressuring the union army by letter to release all confiscated rails. After he got out, one of his first efforts was to get Supt. R.R. Meader to re-lay the rails back toward Fernandina.

The federal government also began repairing the tracks between Gainesville and Cedar Key in July of 1866, but since the trestle to Fernandina had to be replaced, there could be no immediate reinstatement of full operations.

There was a hidden motive in this federal activity. Chief Justice Salmon P. Chase, an ambitious and devious man, had his eye on the railroad. Chase, who had been treasury secretary prior to the court appointment, made a trip to Fernandina in the summer of 1865 and had looked over the terminus. Chase's plan was to have the military rebuild the railroad and turn it over to Lyman D. Stickney, one of his network of former tax agents. (Stickney also had once been indicted for fraud.)

The plot to appropriate Yulee's railroad was uncovered by a former Milwaukee journalist, Harrison Reed--then working as the federal postal representative in Florida--who reported it to Washington. The plot was broken up and Reed later became Florida's governor during Reconstruction.

Chase was a man with presidential aspirations so acute that Lincoln had shifted him out of the cabinet to the Supreme Court to eliminate him as a rival. Chase was still angling for power and tried to build a pro-union loyalist faction in Florida near the end of the war, but it collapsed after the battle of Olustee.

The Reconstruction era in Florida was as nasty as it was in any area in the deep South. The Ku Klux Klan and "regulators" of all kinds terrorized whites and blacks alike, committing an estimated 153 murders in Jackson County alone, according to William Watson Davis. Three attempts were made to impeach Gov. Reed, a conscientious man who included two long-time Floridians in his cabinet, one of whom was the son of James D. Westcott, Yulee's old Senate colleague. Reed was reluctant to re-impose martial law, fearing it would touch off even worse race warfare. But he did ask the federal government for arms to deal with violence, only to have "regulators" seize the guns and destroy them when they arrived.

Consenting to serve in a Reconstruction government meant being branded a "scalawag" if you were a native southerner. But not all scalawags or even all carpetbaggers were corrupt. Reed resisted plundering state institutions as did Ossian B. Hart, another Republican governor who died after a year in office. He and Yulee were good friends.

Hart succeeded Reed and was considered one of the strongest union men in Jacksonville. He served as a federal vote registrar and Supreme Court justice.

Hart played the violin and legend has it that he would play the instrument to calm the alligators behind his home.

In April of 1866, Yulee was elected president and director of the Florida Railroad. He left immediately for New York to raise money to keep the system from being sold. However, the company was unable to keep up its sinking fund payments on bonds guaranteed by the Internal Improvement Fund, so the IIF took over the line in October.

On Nov. 1, the railroad was sold at public auction to Isaac K. Roberts of New York. Three days after his purchase, Roberts deeded the 103 railroad shares to Edward M. Dickerson & Associates after a down payment of $97,800. Dickerson saw to it that Yulee got stock in the reorganized company as well as compensation for past services. Dickerson, however, became president and Yulee vice president.

The railroad offices were once more restored at Fernandina. Yulee and his family moved into a two-story frame house that had served as federal headquarters during the wartime occupation of the town. Plans to extend the railroad down the west coast of Florida to Tampa were once again trotted out. Some grading and preliminary installations had already been completed on the line toward Tampa when the war intervened, but all further work was halted during the war.

By 1868 construction on this leg was resumed. There was even talk of carrying the line as far south as Charlotte Harbor, south of Tampa. The infusion of northern capital got the railroad out of debt by 1869, no small effort in such difficult times.

On Feb. 7, 1870, the Florida Legislature passed an act requiring the Florida Railroad to commence construction of the segment between Waldo and Ocala, with completion due in one year. The railroad's charter was amended to include an extension to Charlotte Harbor and authority was given to issue $3 million worth of capital stock for this purpose. The state also agreed to guarantee certain bonds.

In 1871, the South Florida Railroad Co. was organized to carry out this work and Yulee was named president. An overriding firm, the Atlantic, Gulf and West India Transit Co., was also formed. But in 1875 the courts cancelled the South Florida Railroad Company's contract with the Atlantic, Gulf and West India.

Yulee also managed to get embroiled in a political flap during this period. After the election of 1876, it was charged that the railroad had issued marked ballots to railroad laborers and ordered them to vote or lose their jobs. Yulee claimed the charges were "unfounded and untrue," but curiously added that his company would have been within its rights if it had done what was alleged.

Yulee, the onetime populist, had by now become a conservative, though he declined to re-enter active politics. In 1876 when Florida's vote in a special electoral commission took the presidency away from Samuel Tilden and gave it to

Rutherford B. Hayes, Yulee was a Tilden supporter. The election of Hayes, however, marked the end of Reconstruction and the return of "home rule" to Florida.

Construction of the line to Tampa continued to be easier planned than built. On May 11, 1876, Yulee notified the IIF Board that the Atlantic, Gulf and West India Transit Co. intended to assign the Waldo to Tampa portion to the Peninsular Railway Co. He claimed the line had been under contract twice and "in both instances the contracts were defeated by adverse action in the legislature."

On March 8, 1881 another act of the Florida Legislature created the Tropical Peninsular Railroad Co. and empowered it to build the rail line from a terminus near Ocala to Tampa. Some 44.8 miles between Waldo southward to Ocala were completed by July of 1881.

Tampa newspapers had been critical of Yulee for failing to extend the line to their town, as required by law, but on June 15, 1881 The Tampa Tribune ran an editorial apologizing. It finally looked as if the Tampa connection, which had been talked about for more than 30 years was going to be completed. The editorial was premature, however.

Yulee's organization never did complete the line to Tampa. Only after he sold his railroad interests and the company was reorganized yet again by new investors (into what would become part of the Seaboard Airline Railroad, today known as CSX) did the line enter Tampa. That was in 1889.

Yulee's progress toward Tampa was also blocked by legal difficulties. It was discovered that he couldn't obtain lands granted by Congress in 1856 because rail construction to Tampa hadn't been completed within a 10-year limit set by Congress. Title had reverted to the government It took several years to unscramble this situation.

In 1881, Yulee had finally had enough, selling half his railroad interests to a group of investors headed by Britisher Sir Edward Reed. He left his home at Fernandina and returned to Washington, D.C., where he was welcomed back by politicos who included Lincoln's first vice president, Hannibal Hamlin of Maine; Congressman Hamilton Fish of New York and Congressman Peter Frelinghuysen of New Jersey.

Reed's partners were a mixed lot. They included Dr. Jacobus Wertheim of Amsterdam and Gen. Philip Roddy, a former Alabama cavalry officer residing in London. Reed became president of an organization called the Florida Railway and Navigation Co.

Work continued on the line southward from Ocala. By 1882, it had advanced 15 miles to Wildwood. But in 1885, the Florida Railway and Navigation Co. went into receivership. The receivers were headed by

H.R. Duval, another former Confederate officer whose family was related to Florida's first civilian governor, William P. Duval. Duval was operating the system when, on May 1, 1889, it reached Plant City just outside Tampa. By this time, there were 574 miles of track connecting the Atlantic and Gulf coasts compared to Yulee's original 155.5 miles. Reorganized as the Florida Central and

Peninsular Railroad, it was absorbed by the Seaboard system in 1900.

16

If David Levy Yulee had once believed that Washington's climate was injurious to his health, that thought was far from his mind in 1881 when he returned to the nation's capital. He had regained position and comparative wealth after the Civil War, through 20 years of hectic effort. During this period he had labored unceasingly to bring his railroad back to life. In Fernandina, he was also involved in the real estate business and was part owner of the Egmont Hotel.

In fact, it was at the Egmont Hotel that Yulee entertained President Ulysses S. Grant in 1880. Yulee danced with Julia Grant and Mrs. Yulee danced with the President. She remarked: "Gen. Grant dances beautifully but the music puts him out."

The remark seemed to confirm Grant's reputation for having a tin ear. He once claimed he know only two songs--one was "Dixie" and the other wasn't.

At age 71, Yulee bore himself with dignity. He affected a tall grey beaver hat which added to his 5',7" stature and wore a swallowtail coat. After returning to

Washington he made a $500 contribution to a church at Connecticut and N Streets Northwest, on the condition that no bells be placed in its tower. Undoubtedly this gift was made because he planned to build a home a few blocks away at 18th and Connecticut, today the center of Washington's business area.

The home he built cost $70,000 and the house was considered one of the finest in the city. It was a three-story brick building, with oak-paneled walls, and inlaid wood floors. It was wired for electric illumination, not yet generally in use. It had an elevator, electric servants' bells and speaking tubes. Other features included steam heat with electric thermostats in each room, a wine cellar and a billiard room.

But there was to be no joy in the mansion. Barely two months after they moved in, Nancy Wickliffe Yulee died. Nineteen months later, while returning from a trip to Bar Harbor, Maine, Yulee caught a bronchial infection on the steamboat from Maine to New York. He became chilled when he used his blanket to cover one of his grandchildren, who were accompanying him. Yulee's lifelong fear of the ocean was at last justified. He died on Oct. 10, 1886 at New York's Clarendon Hotel. He had lived 76 years and had labored prodigiously as politician and railroad builder for nearly half a century.

Funeral services were held in Washington at the New York Avenue Presbyterian Church (the same one Lincoln had attended.) David Levy Yulee was buried next to his wife at Oak Hill Cemetery in Georgetown. A marble angel with scroll and uplifted hand was inscribed "they have passed into the Upper Sanctuary." But the inscription also contained an Old Testament allusion that ironically included the name of Yulee's father--the man who had been so torn by his son's departure from Judaism.

It read; "For like Moses & Elias they are conversing of the things that shall come to pass..."

The Washington Post of October 11, 1886 editorialized that Yulee seemed to belong to a "Far-off and almost nebulous period of history." Before the Civil War, the Post noted, "as Senator from Florida he was better known than the state he represented."

The Florida Times-Union of Oct. 13, 1866 said Yulee "probably had a larger influence upon the character and development of the state, and played a larger part in its history, than any other man. He was by far the ablest man that Florida ever sent to represent her in national councils."

There can be no doubt that both Moses Elias Levy and David Levy Yulee were seminal personages in the development of Florida. Certainly the energy which father and son expended in pursuit of their respective goals was hardly to be matched again in Florida's history.

Moses Levy's bold efforts to establish a Jewish homeland and Jewish school might have succeeded had they been begun a few years later. In 1821, Florida was still too much of a wilderness.

As Florida's first builder of a cross-state railroad, David Levy Yulee anticipated by three decades the kind of statewide development which occurred after Henry M. Flagler and Henry B. Plant built their respective railroads in the

1890's, opening peninsular Florida to spectacular expansion. While the capstone of his political career was the transformation of Florida from a wild territory to the 27th state, he functioned always as a wholly American politician, without hyphen, never acting as or on behalf of Jews.

Thus his political record remains a unique and unambiguous one. If the boundaries between his private interests and the public interest were sometimes blurred, if his defense of slavery never wavered, these facts should be judged against the behavior of his contemporaries and his time.

Both Moses Elias Levy and David Levy Yulee were genuine American go-getters in their optimism and persistence in pursuit of their stated goals. Nineteenth century American development took place because a significant number of men were doers who translated their thoughts to action. Moses Elias Levy and his son, David Levy Yulee, belong in that number. They dared.

BIBLIOGRAPHY

BOOKS

BIRMINGHAM, Stephen	"The Grandees, The Story of America's Sephardic Elite," Harper & Row, New York, 1971
BOORSTIN, Daniel J	"The Americans: The National Experience," Vintage Books, New York 1965
BURNETT, Gene M.	"Florida's Past," Pineapple Press Englewood, Fla., 1986
BUTLER, Pierce	"Judah P. Benjamin, American Statesman," Chelsea House, 1873
CATTON, Bruce	"This Hallowed Ground," DoubleDay New York, 1956
COLLINS, LeRoy	"Forerunners Courageous," Colcade Publishers, 1971
DAVIS, Wm. Watson	"The Civil War and Reconstruction in Florida," University of Florida, Florida reprint series, 1964
DERR, Mark	"Some Kind of Paradise," A Chronicle of Man and the Land in Florida," William Morrow & Co., New York, 1988
DOHERTY, Herbert J.	"Richard Keith Call, Southern Unionist," University of Florida Press, 1961
DOUGLAS, Marjory S.	"Florida: The Long Frontier," Harper & Row," New York 1967

DUNN, Hampton	"Accent Florida," Tampa Tribune, 1975
EVANS, Eli W.	"The Provincials, A Personal History of Jews in the South," Atheneum, New York, 1973
	"Judah P. Benjamin: The Jewish Confederate," The Free Press, New York 1988
EPPES, Susan Bradford	"Through Some Eventful Years," University of Florida Press facsimile reproduction of 1926 edition, 1968
FULLER, Hubert R.	"The Purchase of Florida," The Burrows Brothers, Cleveland, 1906
FREUND, Miriam K.	"Jewish Merchants in Colonial America," Behrman House, West Orange, N.J.
HENDRICK, Burton J.	"Statesmen of the Lost Cause, Jefferson Davis & His Cabinet," literary Guild of America, New York, 1939
JAHODA, Gloria	"The Other Florida," Chas. Scribner's Sons, New York, 1967
KORN, Bertram W	"American Jewry & The Civil War," American Jewish Historical Society, Philadelphia, 1970
	"The Early Jews of New Orleans," American Jewish Historical Society, 1969
	"Eventful Years & Experiences: Studies in 19th Century American Jewish Archives, Cincinnati, 1954
LONG, Ellen Call	"Florida Breezes," Ashmead Brothers, Jacksonville, Fla., 1893
McPHERSON, James M.	"Memoirs of American Jews, 1775-1865," (3 Vols.), The Jewish Publication Society of America, Philadelphia, 1955

MARCUS, Joseph Rader — "Memoirs of American Jews, 1775-1865," (3 Vols.), The Jewish Publication Society of America, Philadelphia, 1955

MEADE, Robert Dothat — "Judah P. Benjamin, Confederate Statesman," Oxford University Press, New York, 1943

PATRICK, Rembert W. — "Florida Under Five Flags," University of Florida, 1955

POORE, Ben Perley — "Perley's Reminiscences: Or 60 Years in the National Metropolis," (2 Vols.) Philadelphia, 1886

RERICK, Rowland H. — "Memoirs of Florida," Southern Historical Association, Atlanta, 1902

REZNIKOFF, Charles & ENGELMAN, Uriah Z. — "The Jews of Charleston, A History of an American Jewish Community," The Jewish Publication Society of America, Philadelphia, 1950

STERN, Malcolm — "Americans of Jewish Descent," Hebrew Union College, Cincinnati, 1964

TEBEAU, Charlton W. — "A History of Florida," University of Miami, 1971

THOMPSON, Arthur W. — "Jacksonian Democracy on the Florida Frontier," University of Florida Press, 1961

THESES & MONOGRAPHS

ADLER, Joseph Gary — The Public Career of Sen. David Levy Yulee," Case Western Reserve University, Ph.D. thesis, 1973

ALDERMAN James Leon	"David Levy Yulee, Ante-Bellum Florida Leader (1810-1886)," University of North Carolina, master's thesis, 1980
BROWN, Canter W. Jr.	"The Florida, Atlantic & Gulf Central Railroad, 1851-1868, Florida Historical Quarterly, Vol.69,#4, April, 1991
DODD, Dorothy	"The Secession Movement in Florida," 1850-1861, Florida Historical Quarterly, Vol.III, 1933
HUHNER, Leon	"Moses Elias Levy, Florida Pioneer," Florida Historical Quarterly, Vol. XIX, April, 1941
FAIRBANKS, George	"Moses Elias Levy," Florida Historical Quarterly, Vol. XVIIII, Jan. 1940, No. 3
KORN, Bertram W.	"Judah P. Benjamin as a Jew," American Jewish Historical Society Vol. 38, Pt. 3, 1949
LORD, Mills Minton	"David Levy Yulee, Statesman and Railroad Builder," University of Florida, master's thesis, 1940
THOMPSON, Arthur W.	"David Yulee: A Study of 19th Century American Thought & Enterprise," Columbia University, Ph.D. Thesis, 1954 "Political Nativism in Florida, 1848-60," Journal of Southern History, XV
YULEE, C. Wickliffe	"Senator David L. Yulee," Florida Historical Quarterly, Vol.II, 1909

MICROFILMS

Yulee Papers   P.K. Yonge Library, University of Florida

ARTICLES

MALLORY, Stephen R.   "Last Days of the Confederate Government,"
                             McClure's Magazine, Vol. 16, No. 2,
                             December, 1900

ABOUT THE AUTHOR

Jerald (Jerry) Blizin, a retired Florida journalist, has written on state history subjects for many years. He wrote a column called "Frontier Florida" for the former *St. Petersburg Times* (now *Tampa Bay Times*) and contributed history-based articles to the *Tampa Tribune*, *Washington Star* and *Washington Times*, as well as to magazines. His interest in David Levy Yulee and his father, Moses Elias Levy, dates back more than 50 years.

Made in the USA
Charleston, SC
02 March 2017